A
NEW
VISION

A NEW VISION

*Observations, Experiences and Hopes
for Black People in the Diaspora*

BOLA OGUNKOYA

Matador
9 Priory Business Park
Wistow Road
Kibworth
Leicester LE8 0RX, UK
Tel: (+44) 116 279 2299
Email: books@troubador.co.uk
Web: www.troubador.co.uk/matador

ISBN 978 1784622 046

British Library Cataloguing in Publication Data.
A catalogue record for this book is available from the British Library.

Typeset in 11pt Adobe Casion Pro by Troubador Publishing Ltd, Leicester, UK
Printed and bound in the UK by TJ International, Padstow, Cornwall

Matador is an imprint of Troubador Publishing Ltd

This book is dedicated to my wife, Ade. Without her encouragement, this book would probably not have been completed. It is also dedicated to those Black people who dare to be different and do not conform to the stereotype of what it means to be 'Black'.

INTRODUCTION

The group of friends sat down and somehow the conversation drifted towards their plans, dreams and hopes for the future.

"I want to be a teenage mum living on benefits," said one. Another said, "I want to go to prison."

"I thought we were talking about dreams and the future," said another. "I want to be a drug dealer."

This conversation thankfully did not take place, at least not that I am aware of, however, the vocations put forward will continue to be the only option available for Black people unless we again start to dream, have an understanding of our heritage, our history, our power as a collective and a knowledge as a people of incredible resourcefulness, capability, adaptability strength and compassion.

Before our children and people can start to once again dream and be weaned off a diet of small-mindedness, ignorance and inferiority, we must first ask ourselves: where did we go wrong and how come we are so content with the position we find ourselves in today?

Many will say that the predicament that we find ourselves in today is down to racism, which to some extent is true. However, we cannot continue to blame racism for all of our problems, which unfortunately to some extent are self-inflicted.

Hopefully, this book will be able to shed some light on what we as Black people can do to actually be the people that God intended us to be and not the people that others want us to be.

Many people will probably disagree with many things that I have to say which is fine; disagreement is a good thing as it stimulates debate and conversation which are the key ingredients that give birth to ideas, themes, dreams and action which translates into reality.

However, my hope is that this book will enable people to once again dream, take ownership of their destiny and achieve great things as many of our forefathers did, we need to stop being imitators and start to again be innovators.

We have a great history and once again will have a great future; however this future cannot be forged by relying on welfare or destroying ourselves with gun crime, drugs or violence.

CHAPTER ONE

From the very first moment the Black man set foot on American soil via his forced journey from Africa by way of the slave trade he was never accorded the same rights and privileges as his white counterparts.

He was viewed as a possession and if lucky, part human. Those that had enslaved him were unaware of who he was and what he represented, they were unaware that many of these men and oftentimes children had come from great kingdoms and dynasties, such as the Oyo Empire, the Ghanaian Empire, the Kingdom of Benin etc. Kingdoms that had produced great works of art, such as the bronze works of Benin.

The history books would have us believe that Columbus sailed the ocean blue in 1492, however history, having now been written from a more balanced and objective view as opposed to a Eurocentric point of view, has shown that even before Columbus had dreamed of sailing the ocean blue, Black Africans had already made the transatlantic journey and were already inhabiting the modern day Americas.

In his book *Evidence for an African presence in Early America,* Ivan Sertima talks about Mansa Abubakari II, who launched a voyage that consisted of two thousand ships in 1312. Based on information from a previous voyage that reached the Atlantic, some ships returned and spoke of what they had seen and it was decided to launch a voyage.

The two thousand ships were never again seen. Evidence of this African voyage can also be seen from maps drawn by Europeans that show that the Malians renamed places in the old Mexican region with such names as Mandinga Bay, Sierre de Mali and Mandinga Port, which exist as names of places. Harold G Lawrence's book, *Mandinka Voyages across the Atlantic*, attests to this.

Columbus himself made mention of the fact that he received works of metal of a West African origin from Native American Indians. Incontrovertible evidence shows that 181 years before Columbus 'discovered' the Americas; a Black presence was already there and had already made an impact before he was even born.

Skeletons of two African males were discovered in Hull Bay, near the Danish Virgin Islands and they have been dated to 1250 AD, which shows that Africans were not restricted to the African continent; they were seasoned explorers and travellers.

I make this point as unfortunately, from a historical point of view, too many falsities have been put forward as truth and anything that would put the Black man in a favourable light is hijacked and the Black man is made to look as incapable of making or doing anything good or productive.

As in the case above, many historians would have us believe that the Black man was not capable of possessing the technology to build a vessel that could sail from Africa to America. The same would also apply to the Egyptian pharaohs, and the influence of Egypt's Negroid people which is often overlooked or completely denied.

The same also applies to the beautiful Benin bronzes and the Nok terracotta figurines discovered in Nigeria. Many a historian and archaeologist have gone out of their way to suggest that Black people could not possibly produce such great works of art and instead have tried to attribute some sort of European or Hamitic influence to these works.

The Sphinx of Giza is said to have been built between 7000 BC and 5000 BC. Baron D.V. Denon, a French traveller, commented in 1798 that its features, namely the lips, were African in nature. However, some scholars and academics are still quick to try and denounce the obvious proven craftsmanship of Black Negroid people.

Prior to the coming of the Europeans to Africa, the Black man was actually not doing too badly; he was capable of running great states, kingdoms and empires, he was extremely skilled in working with wood, iron and ivory, he was a great trader (The Trans-Saharan Trade Route), he was religious and had a good relationship with the God of his of forefathers.

He was versed in Architecture, Science, Medicine and the Arts; however all of this was rudely taken away from him when the slave trade suddenly became the most important thing on the minds of the Europeans.

Suddenly, for the next four hundred years or so, the Black man lost all sense of who he was. He was forced to eat new foods, learn new languages and adapt to new customs. Having done this, he still was not accepted in the countries that he now had to call home.

Europe finally ended the slave trade in the 1800s, yet Africa was not given time to recover from her brightest and best being shipped away. She lost manpower and resources and Europe was not eager to give up on a good thing, hence the partition of Africa between 1884-1885. Using extreme violence and brutality, Africa was carved up by Europeans and Europe was now 'legally' able to plunder African resources, as most of Africa came under colonial rule.

Some estimates put the figure of transported Africans to the Americas, Caribbean and other areas at fifty million. Due to the nature of the slave trade, communities were never given the time to recover, as slave traders and in some cases African leaders were always raiding local communities and taking away the strongest and fittest. Family life, agriculture, trade etc. therefore suffered. The transfer of knowledge, experience and education from one generation to the next therefore suffered. To some extent a parallel can be drawn in Western societies, because of the 'modern' life that we live, we now have a generation of adults who cannot cook, do not know how to parent their children or even do basic things such as their own laundry. Parents have failed to pass this knowledge or experience on to their children.

I have yet to meet an African who is able-bodied who cannot cook, do laundry or parent their own children. When I say African, I mean Africans who have not left the continent or do not live in the West, however, I am not sure how long this will continue to be the norm as Western culture and values continue to make inroads into African societies and in our ignorance, we as Africans continue to embrace and consume everything that is Western/European, thinking that it is better than what we have.

Most people would have us believe that the Europeans came and brought order to a continent that had no order or political structure in place – nothing could be further from the truth. Prior to the Europeans coming, Africa was well ordered and run and the Europeans actually wrought disorder and chaos on well run and established kingdoms and empires. Atrocities were committed, such as the Benin massacre of 1897.

Part of the problem that we have is that most things written about Africa have been written from a European/Caucasian standpoint, a lot of rubbish, prejudice and ignorance has been passed off as fact. The views about Africa and its inhabitants have been able to go unchallenged for centuries as Europeans had the advantage of the written word, whereas most African societies were pre-literate and passed their knowledge and experience via oral traditions as opposed to the written format.

Then, as it is today, people were easily seduced by

something they had read and the default position was, and is often, that because something appeared in the print media it must be true.

I remember as a child in the 1970s I was once playing in a field not far from my house, and someone had thrown some bread out to feed the birds. The bread had become stale and I picked up the slices and started to throw them around like a Frisbee. A voice suddenly rang out and said that I should leave the bread alone otherwise I would have my tail cut off. Where did this man get this opinion from? Back then in the 70s, many White people still believed that we as Black people had tails – and why not, when many history books said that we were cannibals, were part human etc.

Till this day I still ask myself why I did not answer. Back then I was known for not holding back. Whether you were a child or an adult, you would remember your encounter with me. Maybe I was just caught off guard or maybe because the man was one of our neighbours and his back garden overlooked the field I was playing in, I don't know.

I also remember a geography class in which the teacher said that people in Africa lived in trees; this was in 1980 and I was in my first year of secondary school. At this point I had not been to Africa, but even I knew that this was not true. I don't know what the other kids thought as I was the only Black child in the class. I didn't really pay too much attention to what was said as the teacher had one leg longer than the other and the nickname we had for him at the time was 'weebles wobble but they don't fall down'.

Contrast the way that the Black man has assimilated and integrated into his new home country(ies) to his White counterpart.

The Black man now speaks English, Spanish, French and whatever language is now spoken in his new home country.

'White settlers' have been in South Africa relatively the same time as the Black men in America, if we are to go with the traditional standpoint of history and yet very rarely will you come across a White South African who speaks Xhosa, Tswana Zulu or Ndebele.The same can be said of any other White population, be it in Canada, Australia, North America etc. these 'settlers' do not speak the language(s) of the indigenous population.

We as Black people are all too quick to give up our sense of identity to become part of societies and communities that still will not really accept us despite the best efforts we make to integrate. When I say give up our sense of identity I am not saying that Black people should not integrate or try and remain separate, I mean that Black people need to have an understanding of what works for them, e.g. strong communities, stable families, good work ethic etc., all of which now seem to have disappeared.

From the above, it can be seen that the Black man, despite his best attempts, is already operating from a position of disadvantage and will continue to do so until he really has a proper understanding of who he is and what he can achieve.

One of the problems we have as Black people is that we have been brainwashed into thinking that everything Western or European equates to being civilized, better or the best and things that have worked for us as Black people are discarded and done away with, such as respect for elders, the extended family system and traditional forms of health care.

I once had a conversation with a friend and although being somewhat facetious his comments had an element of truth to them. He said that if a Black man eats with his fingers he will be classed as a savage, if a White man does the same; it will pass off as having finger food. If a Black man has straw on his dwelling it will be called a mud hut with straw, a White man's abode with straw on the roof will be called a thatched cottage.

Again when the Europeans came to Africa, we were portrayed as savages who wore no clothes and went around naked, however, I have never seen any nudist colonies or beaches in Africa (maybe South Africa). If Europeans want to go for a walk naked or sunbathe naked they are termed as being care free or liberal. If Africans or Black people were to do that we would be termed to be primitive and barbaric.

Health care practitioners in the West who offer a different form of medical care are said to offer alternative medicine or complementary medicine, however, when the same is offered in Africa such practitioners are referred to as charlatans, quacks and backward.

The Harry Potter success/phenomenon is also quite funny. Witchcraft and magic has been given a sanitised Caucasian look and everything is all nice, cute and cuddly, however, if a Black man is to talk about magic, witchcraft or voodoo he is looked upon as being backward and ignorant.

Take for instance the issue of beauty; Black women have for centuries been ridiculed and caricatured for their fulsome lips, breasts and derrières, however, without realising it, others (women) now want to have the attributes of Black women. How many of 'Hollywood's finest' can claim to have natural breasts or lips that are not loaded with collagen or silicone?

If the shoe were on the other foot, the racists and supremacists would be quick to say that we as Black people have an inferiority complex. Why not just give us credit as Black people for having beautiful skin that doesn't have to be nipped and tucked once we pass a certain age. (Those that have looked after themselves, that is). People with darker skin tend to have more melanin and the aging process tends to be slower.

Unless we as Black people can appreciate our own beauty from a Black or African perspective, we will continue to always feel inferior to others. Beauty is universal and no particular ethnic group has a monopoly on beauty.

CHAPTER TWO

One of the areas in which we as Black people have let ourselves down is in the field of education. We have excelled in the field of entertainment and sports, however, we are yet to fulfil our potential in the field of education.

'A mind is a terrible thing to waste' is the slogan of the United Negro College Fund. For the purists of the English Language, some may argue that the slogan should read, 'It is a terrible thing to waste a mind', but whichever slogan you may wish to advocate, the point remains the same; that it is such a shame to let your mind go to waste.

As a young child growing up it was always instilled into me by my father that to be taken seriously, I would have to be twice as good as my White contemporaries. To this effect our house was always filled with books, extra lessons were always on hand, be it English, Maths or handwriting and the library became our second home. I read far and wide and this held me in good stead for years to come. At the time I hated the restriction and limitation on my freedom, as while all my White friends would be out playing football and riding their bikes, I would be at home studying.

However, this limitation was short lived as my father left the UK in 1977 and went to Nigeria to set up his printing business. I became my own boss as my mother now had the unenviable task of raising four children by herself, three of them being boys, and education took a bit of a back seat and was replaced by being pigeon-holed by teachers and silly behaviour on my part.

My father had the foresight to understand that education could and does open up so many doors and therefore from a very early age made it a point of emphasis for his children. Unfortunately, today that is not the case for us as Black people. We have no problem spending £300 on an XBox console or a Playstation console, but we will not spend £300 on books for our children. We have strayed so far that even some Black people will now say that by trying to improve yourself, you are trying to be White. How sad – civilization started in Africa.

Eavesdrop on any conversation that a lot of our kids are having today and you will be shocked. Basic English is not even spoken, you will hear things like "Was you there" as opposed to were you there, "I'm going school" as opposed to I am going to school. I heard a new one the other day, two teenage boys were talking and one said to the other, "I was conversating". I assume he meant to say that he was conversing.

It's one thing to speak slang with your mates, but it's another thing to be able to adjust your speaking and writing to when you find yourself in a formal setting or a business environment, which many of our kids cannot do.

Many of our kids seem to take great delight in showing how ignorant they are. To them they think they are being cool.

If you cannot write or speak basic English how can you expect to get a good job? You cannot plead racism when you yourself are not up to scratch and have not mastered the basics.

People do not know when to use *there* or *their*; *your* or *you're* is a minefield; *hear* or *here* throws up more obstacles.

Fortunately, it isn't just Black kids whose written and spoken English is bad, however, with most negative things, we seem to be over-represented. A lot of white kids also have problems with *should have,* which has now become *should of.* People now say things like, "you should of gone to school yesterday", rather than, "you should have gone to school yesterday". This has happened because of the similarity in sound but without an understanding of what is being said.

Even worse than the bad grammar is the fact that parents and schools alike either do not know the difference or just allow terrible English to be spoken and written.

There are many terrible schools out there with many terrible teachers but this is where we as parents need to step in. We need to instil the importance of education in our children; books not sneakers/trainers and gadgets need to be the most important things. There is no point looking cool if there isn't much going on upstairs.

Standard English needs to be spoken in the home, not all this nonsense that we speak and try and pass off as English. Parents need to be parents to their children, not mates. Censor what your kids watch on TV and what they listen to. (This is not directed to all Black households, however, if the shoe fits.)

If Barack Obama spoke like your typical 'brother' in America, he probably would just about have made it as a janitor at the White House. Guess what, if your speech is littered with, "you get me bruv" or, "I swear down" and you do not know when to switch or how to switch, then already you have placed limitations on how far you will get in your lifetime.

Barack Obama had/has the whole package; he dresses properly, he speaks properly, he had a good education – what is going to stand in his way?

If you walk like one leg is longer than the other and dress like a thug or speak like one, you and not society have already written your history.

We need to embrace education, if you use your mind you can attain great heights; Barack Obama, Colin Powell, Condolezza Rice to name a few.

Too many kids know the things that will not really get them that far in life. They know the latest rap or hip hop record word for word, but ask them what 7 x 7 is or who the first man on the moon was and they look at you as if you've grown two heads.

The irony of the education of Black children as far as the UK is concerned is that nowadays, many Black parents are sending their children back to Africa or the Caribbean for secondary school education, as for one thing, there is a thirst for knowledge and education by children in these areas. The educational authorities are also smart enough to realise that children need guidance, instruction and sometimes discipline unlike in the UK, where children are allowed to beat up teachers, swear at them and excuses are continually put forward for their bad behaviour.

Another problem for Black children is that there are still not enough discernible role models when it comes to the field of education. We now live in a society where intelligence is frowned upon and stupidity, ignorance and crassness are the new vogue.

Television is completely dumbed down, nothing of intellect or importance can be garnered from newspapers, magazines are no different. The gormless and idiotic and cretinous are elevated to superstardom and the only so-called 'success stories' that our kids see are rappers and footballers whose IQ levels at best are also extremely questionable.

Television has now become so corrosive. My generation can remember when a lot of what was shown was educational, whereas today, the majority of programmes shown are for 'entertainment'. I use the term entertainment loosely; what passes now for entertainment is usually quite crass, base and crude.

The majority of films shown in the cinema usually contain quite a high level of violence or sex. Adults and teenagers 'relax' playing video games, many of which again have oftentimes violence and sometimes sexual themes in abundance, and we wonder why we have problems in society.

Why is it that in the space of about thirty years education is no longer seen as a priority for many children and parents in the Black community?

There are so many answers that can be put forward. I don't think that racism per se plays a part, though to some extent it may have some bearing, however, as far as most of the major cities are concerned there is a good mix of children from diverse backgrounds and I believe that as far as a basic education is concerned their needs are met.

Part of the problem, as I mentioned earlier, is that as far as parents are concerned there does not seem to be an understanding of the benefits that a quality education can reap. Many parents are content to let their children rule the roost, discipline is non–existent, parents themselves cannot or choose not to speak properly, bad grammar both verbally and in written form is the norm and children grow up extremely confused because their parents have been lazy in setting a good example.

I think in schools as well, unsurprisingly a number of teachers are totally demoralised and are now just going to school praying that they can just survive the week as opposed to actually teaching and imparting knowledge to their students.

From primary school I have been constantly saying to my son, "don't your teachers correct you when you speak like this?" and the answer would always always be,"no".

The majority of our children now speak an admixture of patois and cockney, which to them is standard English. Unbeknownst to them, if they were to go to any city in Europe and speak like that it would be extremely difficult for them to be understood and they in their ignorance would think that the people they were communicating with were not clever.

Teachers from primary school need to do a lot more to teach our children to speak properly and to pronounce their words properly, slang and ghetto talk needs to stay on the streets and not in the classroom, teaching common sense needs to once again prevail. If children write rubbish, it needs to be highlighted and brought to their attention there and then rather than saying that if a child sees a red mark in his or her exercise book he or she will be psychologically damaged for the rest of their lives.

I think also that the schools in the UK could take a leaf out of the book of schools in Africa. To a certain extent, the school system in the UK is like a conveyor belt system with no quality control; even if a defective product is found on the conveyor belt it is just waved through. In Africa, things are somewhat different. If you fail to meet a certain percentage or grade in your subjects then you repeat the whole year until you reach that standard.

I remember being extremely shocked as a 13-year-old fresh from the UK to the blistering heat of Lagos, Nigeria. My first day at school was an eye opener; the head 'boy' was a giant of a man with a beard. It was only later that I found out that he had allegedly been in the school for ten years, he had apparently spent two years in every class as he was not quite up to scratch academically.

There was no room for silliness in the class. As soon as the teacher entered the classroom we all had to stand up and the teacher, whether male or female, was always armed with the ubiquitous cane and it was used for any minor or major infraction. Many parents will disagree with corporal punishment, however as a former hell raiser I am all for it. Children in the third world go to school to learn not to beat up teachers or for a fashion show. I for one believe that the cane needs to be re–introduced in schools in the UK. (I am also realistic enough to realise that will not happen.)

No parent in Africa would ever dream of coming to school to verbally abuse a teacher or even physically attack a teacher.

Rather, if a parent gets wind of the fact that their child has been disciplined by the teacher they are actually grateful that the teacher cares enough about their child to make them take their studies seriously and you as the child would get a good talking to, if not a warming of the backside for messing about at school.

I can remember children who were so poor that their parents could not afford shoes, coming to school barefooted because they knew the value of education. Even when there was no electricity, students would still have to come to school with their shirts ironed – as they say necessity is the mother of invention, many students would fold their shirts in such a way that when they took it out from under their mattress in the morning the shirt would appear as if it had been ironed. For those of us who were less imaginative, we had to iron our shirts with a coal iron and ensure that not a single black mark appeared on the shirt.

The absence of electricity was never, and is never, an excuse for not doing your homework; you buy a candle or a hurricane lantern and get the job done.

Hard times and tough times are character building and usually are a platform for greater things. Oftentimes, children who come from third world countries and are serious about education usually excel when they come to the West. They have come from an environment where they usually don't have anything, to one where everything is available.

I can remember being in secondary school in Nigeria and the students taking chemistry classes had no chemicals to perform any experiments, yet this didn't quench their thirst for education. My time in Nigeria as far as education was concerned was a wake up call. Even in the 80s, times were hard and many students would have to come home from school, hawk goods like rice or beans to supplement their parents' income, do household chores and then do their homework. Here in the West, people have had it good for so long that there is no need to push or exert themselves. Now that we are in a recession and tough decisions are being made, some of which are right and fair, people are complaining and don't know what to do or how to cope. Many people from third world countries who possess a good work ethic and place an emphasis on education will do surprisingly well during this time and put the indigenous population to shame.

In the 80s Nigeria went through what most of Europe is now going through, the word austerity was introduced into the Nigerian lexicon as well as the acronym SAP (structural adjustment programme) due to the corruption and profligacy of Nigerian leaders. Times were extremely hard, yet we took things in our stride and with good humour. Many families gave up on basics such as milk, eggs and sugar, myself included. Parents asked their children 'have you eaten?' as opposed to 'have you eaten to satisfaction?'

Mathematical formulas were introduced with regards to meals; 1 0 1 meant that breakfast would be eaten and lunch would be missed, followed by the evening meal. Not by choice, but out of poverty, some people had the unenviable formula of 1 0 0 or 0 0 1.

Children in the UK do not know how lucky they are. Education up to secondary school level is free, children from disadvantaged families get free school dinners, books are free, constant electricity and water are the norm in schools, the school building is resistant to all forms of weather and yet with all of this children do not want to go to school.

In my third and fourth year of secondary school, both of my classroom buildings had no doors or windows, the roofs were made from corrugated iron. Nigeria has two seasons, a rainy season and a dry season. Suffice to say that in the rainy season I, like a few other students got wet at times and in the dry season, I became extremely hot.

Some so-called educators have also said students, both Black and White will perform better if lessons were more interesting and fun. I can't say that I share or believe in that assertion. Many children in the third world walk several miles to receive the most basic of education. I've yet to hear it said that such children could not be bothered to go to school because the lessons were not fun and interesting.

Watch your average child in the UK on his or her way to school, the vast majority refuse to wear their tie properly, the shirt or blouse is normally hanging out, make-up and trainers are also part of the school uniform.

If children are not taught to have a sense of self-respect or learn to comply with procedures that are in place then what hope is there? We were all teenagers at some point and the norm is to challenge authority, however, the key is not to give in to such challenges. The key is to explain the reason why such procedures are in place and what benefits can be derived from listening to authority.

In the field of educational achievement Black role models are hard to find and our kids have no one to look up to. I remember growing up as a child and whilst in school, nothing really was taught about Black achievement.We now have Black History Month, which is good, but much more than that needs to be done.

I remember going to Nigeria and meeting members of my extended family and being blown away, there were teachers, doctors, lawyers, accountants, architects, and engineers, PhD holders etc. Back in the UK most Black people worked on London Transport.

Up until that point I had failed to dream, my school report from my school in the UK said that I possessed potential but spent most of my time disrupting the class. Why was I allowed to do that? Because there were no repercussions, anything went and still goes in the schools in the UK. There are lots of Black kids out there in the UK who have so much potential but because the schools do not have any discipline in the classroom these kids get left behind.

Our kids and their parents need to start dreaming. Is it hard? Will it be hard? Of course it will be, as racism will play a part in keeping us down, but we have to realise we are capable of so much more. If things don't work out here, send your kids back 'home' where people understand the importance of education.

In many respects the white community has been smart, they realise and understand the importance of education and to ensure that everything doesn't completely go to pot they have schools like Eton, Harrow and the like.

Even if certain elements of the White community do not want to learn and are happy to live off state benefits, there will always be opportunities for those who want to learn and know the importance of education.

Where is the Black Eton and Harrow? Unless the Black community builds and maintains its own centres of excellence the pace of change for Black people will be very slow. Our Black teachers and educationalists should be looking to create our centres of excellence catering to the educational needs and skills of the Black community. As long as the Status Quo remains, we have to operate from a position of duality, i.e. become adept and sophisticated, educated and politicised in both worlds, Black and White. A lot of the younger generation do not seem to have this ability.

In many respects, we as people of colour have an advantage with regards to operating from a position of duality (that is those who can or those that do).

We are at ease and comfortable operating in the culture that has predominance and our own cultural culture (i.e. other cultures we have been exposed to). Some Caucasian people have a problem when it comes to things like this, not wanting to be classed as racist, some will bend over backwards to the extreme and see issues where no issues exists, others are resentful that other cultures and religions are even considered, while others get it just spot on and are confident, comfortable and experienced with both Black and White people.

Having received a quality education, we cannot look down our noses on those who have not had the same opportunity as us; rather we have to look towards passing the baton on to the next generation.

In America, colleges and universities such as Morehouse, Spelman and Howard University are institutions that are traditionally and historically Black and seek to meet the higher educational needs of such people.

What prevents us in the UK from setting up our own equivalents? Why can we not have our own colleges running in parallel with the existing colleges and universities?

Part of the problem I think is that some Black people do not seem to understand the value of the importance of education or if they do, they have a sort of fatalistic mindset that even if they do get an education, events are so predetermined against them that they still will not get the opportunities that they deserve.

There is a probably an element of truth to that, however, what are the other options? Continue to be disadvantaged and not make any effort?

In the field of education as far as America is concerned, one can see that African-Americans who have a good education can make it to the top. Has it been easy or is it easy? I very much doubt it, but because something is hard or going to be hard should we not strive to make an effort?

The likes of Colin Powell and Barack Obama would not have risen to the heights they have reached if they did not have a good education.

Unfortunately, we in the UK seem to have taken on this crazy attitude that some African-Americans have that striving to have an education or better oneself means that you are trying to be White, which is such a poor way of thinking. For the moment, Africa is credited with being the cradle of civilisation. The University of Sankore in modern-day Mali was built in 1327, Black people really need to know and understand their heritage. Education has always and will always be taken seriously in Africa.

Before Oxford and Cambridge were founded, we had universities in Africa, but these facts are always kept conveniently quiet or not even known by Black people themselves.

Again it goes back to being aware of one's history, if people actually knew the contributions that Black people have made in all walks of life there would be a hunger and desire to continue in the footsteps of those who have gone before.

Education/knowledge is not exclusive to any particular group, race or clan; however, knowledge and education have always been the bedrock of any progressive society.

However, too many in the Black community do not seem to have grasped this. How did we get to the stage where having a good education is now being viewed as a stigma and illiteracy is now seen as being the norm?

In many respects I was fortunate enough to not complete my secondary education in England. I remember getting to Nigeria and meeting many members of my extended family and being extremely shocked that there were doctors, lawyers, accountants and engineers within the family – one aunty even had a PhD in Mathematics.

Growing up as a Black child in a White neighbourhood, my teachers never had any dreams for me, rather the usual stereotypes were on display. If I was to stand up for myself then I was termed to be aggressive, however, I had no problem when it came to sports day, being the only Black child in the school I was always the first to be chosen for the 100 metre sprint. Thankfully, I conformed to the stereotype and was a very good sprinter.

No attention or encouragement was given to me despite the fact that in many areas and subjects I was academically streets ahead of my colleagues. I can remember being in middle school and being in the third group for maths, group one being for the most intelligent and group three being for the less able, even though everything those in group one were doing I was able to do. Why was I in group three?

From that moment onwards, I lost interest in mathematics, so much so that by the time that I got to the final year of secondary school, my interest in maths was non-existent and as soon as the maths teacher entered the class, I would exit the class. Needless to say that I failed my maths O Level on two occasions.

What career advice was given to most people of my age who completed their secondary school education in the UK? What dreams did their teachers have for them? Unfortunately, more often than not, they would be told they aspired to nothing more than stacking shelves in Tesco or working for London Underground.

Nigeria was a different ball game altogether, even if your teachers did not have a dream for you, you as an individual had a dream for yourself. People wanted to become someone or something and do great things with their lives and to that effect would push themselves. Students would set up study groups amongst themselves, teachers would put on extra classes on Saturdays. I can remember forgoing lunch and saving my lunch money to buy books.

With regards to buying books a particular incident is still quite vivid in my mind. I went to buy a book for school called *General Geography In Diagrams* by R.B. Bunnett. Unfortunately, I had not paid attention to the amount of money that I had with me and it transpired that all the money that I had was used to purchase the book. Being about fifteen years of age and not particularly proficient in Yoruba, I was too afraid and proud to ask strangers for money to assist with my bus fare back home. I had gone from my house in Ojota, Lagos to Yaba, Lagos to buy this book. I had no choice other than to walk home in the blazing heat, a distance of about eleven kilometres, almost seven miles.

My predicament was compounded even further by the fact that I took what I thought was a short cut, only to find that the so-called short cut added extra time and distance to my journey. In the long run my journey did pay off as I passed my Geography O Level with a good grade.

From an early age we knew that education was the only way out of the challenging lives that we were living and hence no other choice than to better ourselves educationally was on offer. Africa did and does not have a welfare system whereby if you don't have a job the state will provide for you. The stark reality is if you do not have a job, you do not eat and the best way to get a job is to get a good education.

At present the educational system in the UK – unless you go to a private school – is geared towards mediocrity for both Black and White alike.

Even though we have Black History Month every October, what does it entail? Children are still not given an in-depth education into the achievements of Black people, in many respects it's just another tick box exercise. Are our children being taught about such giants like Paul Robeson, Wole Soyinka, Dr Earl Shaw and Ralph Ellison?

Some organisations also take part very begrudgingly in Black History Month. I recently completed a four month contract at one organisation and one of the employees told me that for Black History Month, the organisation put up posters of Rasta Mouse. Rasta Mouse is a children's T.V. character in which a mouse speaks with a Jamaican accent. If that isn't dumb and insensitive, then I don't know what is. It would have probably been better to not acknowledge Black History Month than come out with such rubbish.

Unfortunately our children's minds and brains are bombarded and saturated with such mediocrity through the media that they are quite happy to aspire to be like a lot of the gormless Black people they see on TV, or in the more extreme cases, the local drugs baron or gunman.

We need to go back to the very fundamental basics of education whereby right from primary school, children and teachers alike need to be taught to speak and write properly. The word *three* should be pronounced as such and not *free*. *With* pronounced as *with* and not *wiv*, *youth* as *youth*, not *yoof*, the list is endless. If you speak like someone who hasn't really paid much attention to their education you cannot complain when job opportunities do not come your way. Parents especially have an important role to play here, our kids did not fall out of the sky at age sixteen, we have had an opportunity to coach them, raise them and nurture them from the very beginning. Unfortunately, many parents have forgotten that once a child arrives, it's time for the partying and all-night drinking sessions to stop.

Becoming a parent involves sacrifice, sacrifice of time, money etc. Many parents believe that with the arrival of their children, no adjustments need to be made to their lifestyles and they can continue to live like single people without a care in the world, absolved of any responsibilities.

Not having invested any time in teaching or educating their children or even setting an example for them –a good one at least– they start to shed tears when suddenly their children are being locked up or even being buried having just barely reached puberty. One has to ask the question, where were you when your child was growing up? What morals did you instil in him or her? You as a parent are the primary teacher and educator of your child, it is not the job of the state, social services or teachers to raise your kids, it is your job and your job alone!

I am aware of the fact that some children even though they are taught the difference between wrong and right will still go off the rails, but this is still not an excuse to not make an effort, we only get one chance to get it right with our children and therefore cannot afford to leave anything to chance. If we allow a void to be created, something will take the place of that void, i.e. the gunman or drug dealer.

I also strongly believe that if children have not reached a certain level of proficiency at school they should be made to repeat the year. How can a country such as England that once was a beacon of education to the world now be at a stage that after eleven years of 'education' children can leave school without being able to read or write properly or in some cases not at all?

Teachers need to be given the right to create a conducive atmosphere for learning within the classroom and if that involves corporal punishment so be it. For those of us that were quite wayward at school, myself included, a bit of physical punishment did us no harm; in fact, in hindsight I am grateful that my teachers cared enough to discipline me when I needed it.

Today, in England, children rule the classroom, teachers are undermined, beaten up and in some cases have been raped and killed all in the name of this crazy and destructive liberalism that has come to replace common sense and decency.

When teachers do try and defend themselves from such attacks, it is deemed to be assault and oftentimes results in prison sentences and destroyed careers and lives on the part of the teachers and yet successive governments fail or refuse to see the correlation between a breakdown in discipline in the classroom and the stunted educational development of children, especially Black children.

I recently walked past a secondary school in Kennington in South London and was quite dismayed at what I saw – about 95% of all the children in the playground were Black. I asked, myself where are all the White children? Kennington has a good mix of both White and Black people, so why should this school be predominantly Black.

The phrase 'White Flight' came to mind, I don't think the people who live in Kennington are racist, that is the parents of the White children, however, they probably have cottoned on to the fact that a school that is predominately Black is probably going to have lower standards in everything from expectations, to discipline, to educational standards.

To some extent I felt sorry for the children as I thought already all the chips are stacked against them. How in a city like London can you have a school that is about 95% Black, if we were in Lagos or Kingston, Jamaica that would be understandable. What kind of education will be given to these children?

Having said that though, to some extent we, parents and children, still need to rise up to the challenge and go the extra mile and put in the additional hard work ourselves. Study groups can be organised, visits to the library can be made and books can be invested in.

There was a saying that I heard recently, which to a certain extent has an element of truth to it. "If you want to hide anything from Black people, put it in a book because Black people don't read."

Black people do read, however, I think a lot of Black people read the wrong things a lot of the time. Most of the time our people are reading the wrong kind of material, a lot of the things that are being read are the same old things, books about a cheating spouse and the usual negative stereotypes of Black people, worst of all a lot of these books are written by Black people as well.

What is wrong with reading a book about history, politics, science, art, geography? We need to get away from this destructive and negative mindset that trying to improve oneself or get an education is equivalent to trying to be White.

We unfortunately now live in a world where getting a proper education is no longer a priority. We are bombarded and assaulted visually and the superficial and fleeting reality of 'celebrity' is what our children now aspire to.

We now find ourselves in a situation where children leave school, and sometimes college, still not able to read or write properly, they are bereft of common sense, they have no social skills and yet they still believe that the world owes them everything.

Unless we get back to placing an emphasis on education, the future for Black children is extremely bleak.

Rather than pushing the "urban" agenda – code for being hip, ghetto and ignorant – why are we not pushing the education agenda?

A society that rewards crassness, stupidity over intelligence and hard work only has itself to blame when things start to fall apart.

The question is often asked, what does it mean to be Black?

We don't ever seem to ask what does it mean to be White or Asian, however, the sad thing is that if we were to ask Black people what it means to be Black, I fear the results might not be to favourable. Many Black youth or teens I doubt would equate Black with being articulate, intelligent or educated. Many would consider a very negative image of something like a 'bad boy' to be a representative of what it is to be Black.

It is often said that a girl gets her image of what a man should be like or what a relationship should be like from her father, however, in the Black community where are the fathers who should be setting an example for our young girls? Too often many dads are not there, leaving young girls with no real understanding or knowledge of how they should be treated in a relationship.

Single parent households are on the increase and oftentimes young girls do not even know who their fathers are and more often than not, gravitate to the first male that shows them a bit of attention. These young males themselves at times are emotionally stunted and not really understanding what it means to be a man. In some cases ignorance, violence and petty theft are usually what they bring to the relationship, which does not bode well for the relationship itself or any offspring that may come into the partnership. Education as well, at times, has also taken a back seat and the cycle of disadvantage continues.

There also appears to be a vacuum where magazines or periodicals targeted for the Black community is concerned. Magazines and periodicals that will challenge inspire and inform. We have magazines for hair, music etc., but I am yet to come across any, at least in the UK anyway where current affairs, politics etc., are aimed at the Black community.

As a teenager in Nigeria, I remember having to save up for my regular fix of *Ebony* and *Right On* magazine, which was great, but that only catered to one aspect of my personality, there is so much more to Black people than music, sport and hair.

Magazines came and went, I remember a magazine called *South* which dealt with issues on the African continent, but its longevity was short lived. We all know about *TIME* and *News Week* and *Readers Digest*; where are the Black equivalents? Why are magazines that are not Black owned going to write about Black issues? It's not a matter of being racist, the target audience they write for appear to have broader interests.

Having not bought *Ebony* magazine for many years, I purchased a copy recently and I was disappointed. Most of the magazine was dedicated to adverts and letters and the odd interview here and there. I think *Ebony* can do more.

Recently a friend of mine rang in a bit of a rage; he lives in Ilford which is a predominately Asian area. He had just come back from collecting his daughter from Sunday extra-curricular lessons and was angry that his daughter was the only Black child there, as opposed to all the other Asian kids.

He felt that we as Black people are too lazy to make the effort to get our children into extra lessons and that the gap between our children and White/Asian children is widening in terms of educational achievement and aspiration.

The conversation that we had lasted over an hour, however, while I agreed with some of the things he said, I informed him that he was looking at things from too simplistic a point of view. Extra lessons cost money, most Asian families will probably have two parents at home and have a good extended family network. A lot of Black families cannot say the same.

Unfortunately, we in the Black community seem to take our cue from America, we are constantly bombarded by music videos that glamorise violence, misogyny and the bling lifestyle. To many youngsters, success is not about being able to read or going to college or university, it's about making fast and easy money and living the instant gratification lifestyle. No other people or group have to contend with such images being imprinted into the psyche of their children.

No other people have a history quite like ours, for centuries we have been denied access to education. Yes, slavery ended many years ago, but its effect and trauma did not. For hundreds of years, it was illegal for African-Americans to read and those caught reading would be severely punished if not killed.

Even when we have gone out to get an education, many people have found themselves unemployed and just not given the opportunity to progress, so to the younger generation they do not feel the need to get an education as people who have done that are still struggling to make headway.

If you are denied access to education, political processes, legal redress, public finances and for hundreds of years have to fight to prove your worth as a human being, then even the most basic things will prove to be difficult. Can Black people do more for themselves? Most definitely, however, it is a bit too simplistic to say we are lazy; our history is unique and extremely complicated.

However, if we as a people give education the priority it deserves, I believe a noticeable change will occur in the Black community.

CHAPTER THREE

I was lucky enough to be born towards the tail end of the 60s, so as a teenager and a young man I got to hear the great music of the 70s and 80s and some of the 90's. Oftentimes today, the name of an artist or a track will suddenly come to mind and I'll quickly look it up on YouTube and great memories will come flooding back.

A friend and I have actually said that if we ever win the lottery, our plan is to open a nightclub solely dedicated to eighties music. I hope it happens as we are getting on a bit.

Music is such a powerful tool and medium and its power can never be underestimated, one only has to look at the impact of such events as Live Aid to recognise and understand the power and influence of music.

Even in Biblical times, we are told that when Saul was troubled by an evil spirit, he would call upon David who would play the harp for him until he was relieved of his torment.

I was fortunate to move to Nigeria at the age of thirteen and would spend almost ten years there before returning to the UK.

Musically, those ten years were the best ten years of my life, I was treated to the best of 'Black music' that there was on offer. Those were the days when you would have the 7" version of a song, an acappella version, 12" version, club mix etc.

Going to parties, there were certain tracks that if you had not played, you couldn't claim to have had a party, such as 'Nightshift' by the Commodores or 'The Finest' by the SOS Band, 'Treat her like a lady' by the Temptations. Other tracks that come to mind are 'Let's start over' by Miles Jaye, 'Who do you love' by Bernard Wright, 'Lovin' you' by Ray Parker Jr, 'Rhythm of the night' by Debarge, the list would also not be complete without adding 'Make that move' and 'Night to remember' by Shalamar.

Other tracks to get everyone on the dance floor would be 'Fools Paradise' by Meli'sa Morgan, 'It's Your Night' by James Ingram, 'Here I am' and 'Check it out' by Dynasty. When it came to slow numbers, who could forget tracks like, 'Shadow Lover' by the Mary Jane Girls or 'You don't have to cry' by Rene and Angela, 'Feels so Good' by Midnight Star or James D-Train Williams', 'Oh how I Love You (Girl)'. I could go on and on and on. The sad thing is that there isn't a market for such music or singers anymore, or if there is it is ignored.

Fast forward twenty, thirty years and you have to ask yourself; what has happened to 'Black music'? The music, if you can call it that, seems to have regressed and not progressed, song writers have become lazy and the majority of singles and CDs come with an advisory label on them (not all of today's 'Black' music is not quite up to scratch, but a great deal leaves a lot to be desired).

To cover for their mediocrity, record companies will quickly cobble together a video with a few semi-naked women and suddenly we have a 'hit 'on our hands.

Talent has suddenly given way pretty much to soft porn. Today anyone can play a few chords and put together a few repetitive beats, get together a few girls in bikinis and suddenly they are an artist with a hit single on their hands.

I think back to the music I listened to back then as a teenager and young man and I cannot really think of any records that were labelled 'parental guidance' or 'explicit lyrics'.

Even if a song was a bit rude or saucy it was done in such a tasteful way that the song was still enjoyable. Marvin's Gaye's

'Let's get it on' or Ray Parker Jr's 'I don't think that men should sleep alone' really don't leave much to the imagination as to what the intention is, however, you would never refer to them as being rude, crass or filthy.

Sex and violence are the main themes of most of what we would call Black music today and the mass media is all too complicit in shoving these images in our faces.

It is quite sad that records that refer to women as 'bitches' and 'ho's' can become hit records, one has to ask what has happened to our moral compass and direction? Why do we in the Black community feel the need to put down our women, do we see such negative and destructive behaviour in the White community?

Is it any wonder that the Black community is imploding on itself when a lot Black men have no respect or regard for women and a lot of Black women in turn think negatively about a lot of Black men? We have a situation where many Black households do not have a father figure in the home. It is not a crime to be a single mum and many single mums out there are doing a great job, however, you don't need to be a rocket scientist to figure out that generally children from a two-parent household do better than children from a single parent household.

Children from a single parent household, where the mother is White probably have a better chance than children in the same situation whose mother is Black as, generally speaking, White women will be better off financially than Black women.

Children growing up in these single parent Black households from an early age are already at a disadvantage. From quite early on some Black boys are told that all men are dogs and some Black girls are constantly hearing how useless Black men are, neither party has any real incentive to try and correct this misconception.

Recently, I listened to a radio show where the host was asking why a lot of Black women seem to be dating white men. A Black lady who was dating a White male rang in to say that her choice of partner was down to the fact that she felt he would be faithful. No one race has a monopoly on fidelity, however, as I am sure with other races, there are more than enough Black men out there with several different children with several different partners.

Black parents also have a vital role to play in monitoring what their children listen to and watch on TV. Oftentimes it's all too easy to dump the kids in front of the TV and let them get on with it.

So many children today are spoilt and overindulged and have TVs and PCs in their bedrooms with no regulation on viewing or enforced bedtimes. Is it any wonder why children are growing up too fast and seeing things and listening to things that they probably shouldn't?

I have seen so many bad examples of parents blasting age inappropriate music with their very young children in the back and you just have to ask yourself: with irresponsible and selfish parents like these, what chance do these kids have?

If you want to listen to that kind of expletive laden music, why subject your children to it? Many of these children will grow up and be able to curse you fluently, but will not be able to string together a proper sentence in spoken or written English.

One only has to look at how things have changed with regards to going to a night club. It almost seems to be the norm now when a shooting or stabbing happens, it happens in places where there is a predominately Black crowd and predominately 'Black music' is being played.

'Black music' today in the main has, in many respects, dumbed down our children and desensitised them.

Our music has lost its way and is also taking our children to a very horrible and dark place.

The irony of the whole gangsta rap/hip hop music scene is that it is not the Black community that is benefitting from the financial proceeds. Record companies and labels in the White community are those that are benefitting. In many respects it is rap and hip hop that has sold out, the lifestyle that it portrays is out of reach for the average kid in the hood. Rappers and the like have no problem flaunting their wealth in front of everyone, but why not do something really beneficial and tangible with it. Regenerate a community or a neighbourhood.

In 1988 Bill Cosby donated twenty million dollars to Spelman College in Atlanta, America. Education opens a lot more doors than hip hop ever will. Like some of the bankers we hear about, rappers and the like spending hundreds of thousands at a night club – but who really benefits from that? Yes, it's a great ego trip, but it pretty much stops there. How many lives has Bill Gates saved or improved by his generosity? From health programmes to educational programmes, Bill Gates has used his wealth to make a difference, especially in places like Africa.

A lot of rappers etc. may be very well off financially, but what they don't understand is that, apart from money, you need to have influence or political clout to get things done, from the abolition of slavery to the fight for gay marriage, White people have been the ones with the power and the influence to effect change. To get that kind of influence, and power, you generally find education playing a very prominent role, something that we as a people need to excel in.

You can have all the bling and money but if you cannot think or express yourself to a wider audience, things will be difficult. The scary thing is that a lot of people believe that once they have money, nothing else matters. Money will buy you a lot of yes men and women, but once the money has gone, life becomes a lonely place. Too many people that have 'made it' have suddenly lost it all. Maybe better education and a bit more common sense would have enabled them to hold on to their fortunes. Too many of our people have fallen into this trap.

Musically, a lot of Black people miss out as they believe that if they only listen to 'Black music' then that is enough. If you listen to rock or punk then you are a sell out.

Music is universal and no one genre is better than the other. In my CD collection I have albums by the Beach Boys, Blondie, Kings of Leon, Roxy Music and the Police, to name a few.

My wife, who is half-Jamaican and half-Nigerian, loves her Country music – yes Country music – she loves her Dolly Parton, Kenny Rogers, Don Williams and the like.

I must admit her taste in music did throw me, as while I felt my taste in music was broad and varied I had never met a Black person who was into Country music. The beauty of it all is that our house is always filled with the sound of different styles and genres of music and my son is growing up with an appreciation for good music both 'Black' and 'White'.

If you want to hear a great love song, listen to Barry White, Luther Vandross, Teddy Pendergrass or Freddie Jackson, those guys knew how to sing a song and really get you in the mood in a classy and sophisticated way. Who out there today is doing justice to Soul music or R&B?

In defence of their music, these so called artists/singers will say that they are just keeping it "real" and singing about what is going on in the streets or in their environments, which to a certain extent could be true, however, are we to believe that there is never a positive thing going on to sing about?

Is it all doom and gloom 24/7, 365 days a year? I would have to disagree, even when racism was very much alive and well in America, people still sang, spoke and wrote of hope, positive messages were still put forward, people didn't keep it "real" by turning on themselves and trying to destroy their own kind.

As I am typing, I am actually listening to Tina Turner's 'River Deep Mountain High', prior to that I listened to Marvin Gaye's 'What's going on'. Even back in the sixties our music was so beautiful, passionate, soulful, powerful and moving, it really did touch your soul, it elevated you, transported you, mesmerised you and put you on a natural high. I can't really say that about today's "Black music".

How low have we fallen that today, a good time cannot be had without having to get drunk or high on drugs and then end the night dodging bullets or evading the slashes of someone armed with a knife trying to settle a score over a perceived slight.

In our music of yester year, you could hear real instruments being played, real musicians played a part in putting together a hit record and great masterpieces were produced.

Shows such as the X-Factor, American Idol and Pop Idol are the new breeding ground for future singers. These shows in themselves are not bad as some people who do have real talent have actually come through and have gone on to have a measure of success, however, these shows in a sense are not really preparing people for the reality of life in the music industry.

Because we now live in a world where everything is based upon how you look with no relevance given to anything else, people believe that if you look good and can prance about in a skimpy outfit or have your six pack on display then automatically you have all the credentials to be a recording artist.

Judges on these shows don't really do much to help the cause, oftentimes after a performance is given, judges will say things like "you look amazing". However, no comment is made about the actual performance.

Whilst the emphasis is placed on looks and not talent, our children are already placed at an automatic disadvantage because the concept of beauty is still portrayed as a Western or European ideal, so to get attention our children have to settle for the next best thing which is usually an 'urban' look or sound.

Before his untimely death Michael Jackson was probably one of the few artists who could rely solely on his music to get the attention of his audience. He didn't have to strip off or have skimpy dancers on stage to compensate for his lack of talent. He had the talent in bucket loads as a dancer, songwriter, singer, performer and producer.

Today, there seems to be a limitation placed on "Black music" or artists. Almost every Black singer is automatically labelled as either a hip hop star/rapper or R&B singer. If Jimi Hendrix were alive today, what box would we put him in? "Sail On" by the Commodores apart from being a great song in many respects is very "Country". Over the years "Black music" has changed and different genres have come and gone from funk to new jack swing to name a few.

If we have run out of ideas or are running out of ideas, there is no harm in looking backwards, there is a lot of great material out there that was amazing in its day.

Are we too far down the line to return to good clean wholesome lyrics in the music our children listen to? Only time will tell.

CHAPTER FOUR

Racism is described as antagonism or discrimination towards other races.

With regards to race and crime, America has a shocking and appalling record. In his book, *Race, Crime and the Law*, Randall Kennedy details one of hundreds if not thousands of injustices carried out against Black people in the United States.

A slave called Sam was beaten for being drunk, the slave was whipped by his master and then was whipped by another man when his master became tired, he was washed with hot water which had had peppers infused in it. The slave was also stamped on, needless to say, the slave died.

It is easy to think that miscarriages of justice only happened in the times when slavery was alive and well and racism was often disguised as 'wrong doing' – nothing could be further from the truth. The Los Angeles riots sparked by the acquittal of police officers that beat Rodney King exposed probably what was already known but not acknowledged – the entrenched racism of the Los Angeles Police Department.

America has a history of brutalising and stigmatising its Black citizenry. Progress has been made in the fight against racism; however, there is still a long way to go. Some White people still view Black people as 'problem people' not knowing or acknowledging the wrongs that have been committed against Black people; they have no idea of the disparities or inequalities Black people face.

From substandard housing underfunded education,

neglected neighbourhoods to drug ravaged communities, Black people have to contend with more than almost any other group in America.

Rather than viewing us as problem people, see us as people who have had problems thrust upon us. Of all the people that have come to America, the Black man was the only one who arrived in chains, had no rights and was viewed as a possession and a threat. The physical chains may no longer be apparent, but we are still chained emotionally, psychologically, and in so many other ways. The fate of America's native population is also well documented, the common denominator in both how Blacks and the Native population have fared and both being treated by the "immigrant" Caucasian population.

Are all Caucasians bad? No. Can the impact of America's Caucasian populace on the current predicament America's Native population and Black people find themselves in today be discounted? No.

To those who have made it, special praise and recognition must be given as the challenges and obstacles they have faced have been immense, the history of most Black people is one of being disenfranchised, raped, robbed, marginalised, deprived, excluded, incarcerated, etc. To have overcome and succeeded shows the resilience and determination of the spirit of the Black man and woman.

Blacks picked the cotton in the fields, raised the families of Whites, fought wars in foreign lands only to come back home to be told to sit at the back of the bus or use separate washrooms and against this backdrop we have produced great intellectuals, four star generals, a President, entrepreneurs etc.

England fares no better in regards to acknowledging it's debt to Black Africans, the West African Frontier Force made up of troops from Nigeria, Ghana, Gambia and Sierra Leone fought for the British Empire in the 1st and 2nd World Wars as well as in Burma in 1953. What recognition has been given for their sacrifices? Nigeria's contribution to the WAFF was about 45,000 men – it is said that 8 out of 10 soldiers who fought in Burma were Black.

When Remembrance Day is marked, what mention is made of these men, how many even know of the West African Frontier Force? Mention is made of the Ghurkhas and their sacrifice, but the bravery and sacrifice of the men of the West African Frontier force is conveniently forgotten.

It just goes to show that we can rise above any adversity and still accomplish amazing things. What helped us to achieve this? Family, standards that we had and the culture we brought from the Motherland. Unfortunately all of this has been eroded and broken, hence the predicament we now find ourselves in today.

We have forgotten our history and our heritage. Our family and religion is now Nike, games consoles, Blackberry and Facebook.

If one thinks critically or logically, then one can only describe racists as being incredibly stupid or evil. Why would you hate someone or a particular group of people because they look different to you?

Racism should not be confused with ignorance, there are many people who are ignorant of other races and people and say a lot of stupid and unwise things. A perfect example being an incident that occurred when I once visited my sister many years ago.

My sister lives in a predominately White neighbourhood, as her husband is White. She introduced me to one of her neighbours who happened to be White and the lady said to me how come you are a different colour to your sister, she was inferring that I was of a darker complexion to my sister. (I was at that time.)

Was the lady racist? No. Was it a dumb question? Yes, anyone who knows anything about Black people will know that even siblings from the same mother and father will not all be the same complexion. However, this lady was speaking from her limited exposure and experience with Black people so it would have been naïve and childish of me to take offence with her.

If the roles were reversed and I were to ask a White person, why do you have blue eyes and your sister has grey eyes, would that be a racist question? No, but it would be a dumb one as we all know that White people all have differing eye colours, blue, grey, hazel brown etc. and the same goes for hair colour.

Great strides have been taken in the US and UK with regards to combating racism. However, in this politically correct age that we live in, when allegations of racism are made they are sometimes not dealt with as robustly as they should be, because when you get to the heart of the matter you usually find out what has been alleged to be racist is usually ignorance and not racism and at times racism is pleaded to cover up incompetence.

Does that mean that racism does not exist? Far from it, from the moment the Black man 'left' the continent of Africa and took up residence in Europe, South America, etc., he was discriminated against, oppressed, denied basic human rights and killed simply because he looked different.

It would be too simplistic to say that all White people are racists, as that would not be true and is not true. However, one does have to ask why it is that in countries that were not originally the countries of White people; Australia, South America, The Caribbean, Canada, America, South Africa etc., the indigenous populace do not seem so antagonistic to these recent 'settlers'.

I could be wrong, but I don't know if any of these countries or territories have a political party or pressure group that wants to deny citizenship or repatriate these 'White settlers' to their country of 'origin'.

In the US, the KKK had the audacity to discriminate against Black People. At the turn of the 20th Century the majority of Black People in American were American born. One also has to ask why is the KKK not seen and labelled as a terrorist organization? This is an organisation that killed and terrorised many Black people.

In the UK we have the BNP, a not very pleasant 'political party' whose main aim is to repatriate all people of colour to their country of 'origin'.

In the UK, there has been a huge influx of immigrants from Eastern Europe and this has brought about tension in some communities. However, as I pointed out recently to a friend, in about 25-30 years time these immigrants and their children will have become assimilated and acculturated in to UK society and the focus will turn away from them onto Black people again, as unlike Eastern Europeans we tend to stand out in a society that is predominately White.

People to some extent hold racist views because they have no understanding or knowledge of history. Now that many people, both legal and illegal, are coming to the UK we are told that many of the refugees are in fact not refugees but economic migrants. However, if we cast our minds back to the 1800s, the same thing happened in Ireland. The Irish potato famine led many families to flee Ireland and head to America for a better life and better opportunities. They too were economic migrants. Also, many Europeans went to America – without Visas, mind you – and took up residence in America as they were fleeing religious persecution. They changed the racial landscape forever. Where is the Native American Indian today?

In the main contained in a reservation with a few casinos on the land that his forefathers owned that has kindly being 'gifted' back to him by the American Government.

When the Europeans landed in America, the Native American helped him to till the land, as he had no concept how to cultivate the land – his kindness and accommodation was not met with the same from the Europeans.

There are immigrants in the UK but despite all the scaremongering about being swamped, I doubt we will ever change the racial landscape as the Europeans did to the Americas.

The Slave trade saw millions of Africans ferried to the Americas and the Caribbean, they didn't change the landscape of the countries they were taken to as they were still in the minority and some countries in the Americas made sure that even if this were a possibility it would never become a reality. I have often asked myself why is it that most countries in South America have a sizeable Black population bar Mexico and Argentina? Argentina employed a form of ethnic cleansing to rid itself of Black people. Many Black Argentines were made to fight in the Argentine War of independence of 1810–1818. Black Mexicans fare no better today, they are constantly harassed by the police and some Mexicans themselves do not know they even have a Black population.

Race and crime is another area where unfortunately racism and stereotyping play a big part. Admittedly, we do have a problem, especially in London with teenage gangs armed with knives and guns. Oftentimes when a shooting or stabbing has happened, you will hear stupid comments, such as "send these people back to where they came from". Nine times out of ten, 'these' people are British born. Where do we send them to? Their actions must be rightly condemned, but why inject racist comments into the argument?

When a White paedophile has abused a child, the appropriate condemnation is made, but who is asking for 'these' people to be sent to where they came from? The UK is an island, so surely they and their ancestors came from somewhere else, are we not all foreigners to this country? It should also be noted that the majority of paedophiles in the UK are White, but that fact never seems to be picked up by the media or if it is, colour never seems to come into the equation when the story is reported. If and when a Black paedophile is caught, then we will start to hear the same old tired phrases, "What is wrong with those people" (those people being Black people, not paedophiles) or "Those people need to be sent back to where they came from."

Another recent phenomena, or maybe not so recent, just more reported, is the number of teachers having sexual relationships with their students. It seems like almost every month there is a story of a teacher caught having sex with students, even worse, there also seems to be an increase in paedophiles molesting children in nursery school. Again, the majority if not all involved happen to be White.

In these cases, the crime and not the ethnicity is the focus, however, the Black and Asian community do not have the same luxury when 'specific' crimes are carried out by certain members of their community. More often than not an entire race or ethnic group is condemned and not the crime.

With regards to gun crime, we will hear things like the Black community needs to sort out its gun crime issue. Likewise, we also hear things like the Asian or Muslim community needs to deal with Islamic extremism. I have yet to hear that the White community needs to deal with its paedophile issue.

Crime is not race specific, there are White and Asian gun men as well as Black and Asian paedophiles, but again it is always to someone's advantage to try and attribute certain crimes to certain groups, thereby allowing ignorance, extremism and racism fertile ground to spread.

The *News of the World* newspaper closed after 168 years of being in business due to its despicable and disgusting behaviour of hacking into peoples voicemails. The action has been rightly condemned, however I am sure if a Black person, be it editor or reporter had done this, I do not think it would just be their actions that were condemned.

Racism today is now very covert and subtle and as my friend Segun says, "if you blink you'll miss it".

Quite a few years ago a Black British Olympic sprinter was said to have tested positive for a banned substance. Many of the Newspapers had a field day reporting the story, suddenly this Black British sprinter who had won a number of medals for the country was now referred to as Jamaican born.

When he was winning medals for the UK and taking the Union Jack on laps of honour, why was he not referred to as Jamaican born then?

Recently, I read a report in a newspaper with regards to Serena Williams, which I thought was very racist in a very subtle way. The reporter went on to say how Serena had blasted and barged her way through the match. No mention had been made of some of the great rallies that took place during the match.

You can't just blast your way through a match, there is a certain element of skill that also comes into play, but this is never made mention of when some reporters want to write about the Williams sisters.

Many people do not really have an understanding of the impact of racism; people have lost careers, housing and an opportunity to progress merely because of the colour of their skin.

Imagine going to university to better yourself but being unable to procure employment just because you look different.

Imagine being denied the opportunity to get accommodation, not because you cannot afford to pay the rent but because you look different.

Any person of colour will tell you what it feels like to walk into a shop or department store and suddenly the security guard or staff want to become your best friend and decide to follow you around the store.

Why would people make such assumptions about others without getting to know them? Any person that I meet irrespective of colour, I do not make any assumptions about them until I get to know them properly. Such an individual has to give me reason to not trust them or like them, I will not automatically just jump to that conclusion.

If I meet a White person, I will not assume because they are White that they must be racist or that their great, great-grandfather was a slave trader.

I will not assume than an Asian man is automatically a shopkeeper or that a Chinese man must own or work in a Chinese takeaway. Why are we as Black people not given the same benefit of the doubt?

Because you are Black, people automatically assume that there is a certain way that you must walk, talk and dress. Unfortunately, this assumption is held by both Black and White people.

I once spoke to a woman on the phone and we had a very interesting conversation, as I had introduced myself, she said my name was quite unusual and asked quite innocently – as is often asked – where I was from. Though being born, bred, buttered and toasted in the UK I refer to myself as being Nigerian. It just makes things a bit easier as people always say that's a strange name, where's that from, it's just easier to say I'm Nigerian.

She commented that I sounded very English; I knew

exactly where she was coming from but decided to play dumb, I informed her that I was born in England and shouldn't sound anything other than English.

What she was alluding to was that I didn't sound 'Black'", I sounded 'White' and spoke standard English. I found it quite sad that probably this lady had never come across Black people who spoke standard English who could pronounce words properly and had a good command of the English language.

Her experience of Black people was probably what people in today's parlance would be described as being urban, street or ghetto.

Racism in part I think is perpetuated by the labels that new arrivals or non White English/British people are given. Ethnic minorities – what a horrible and non-inclusive title to give anyone. Is it any wonder why native born non-Whites still feel a certain sense of alienation when they are not simply just referred to as British? Who wants to be classified as a minority in their country of birth/naturalisation? The word minority itself conjures up so many negative connotations, i.e. such as not really belonging or being a part of.

The Americans to an extent have dealt with this issue, at least everyone is considered to be an American, i.e. Native American, African-American, Irish-American, Italian-American, etc. Everyone is made to feel like they have a stake in the country as they are all Americans.

Imagine having no affiliation to the country of your birth as you are not even categorised as a citizen, you are an ethnic minority. It almost comes across as though we are some kind of threat.

Politicians must also take some blame as to the way that non-White people are treated in this country and the perception that some White people hold about people of colour.

The politically correct culture/agenda in my mind has worsened race relations: how can we have situations where in some schools, Christmas is not celebrated or 20-30 different languages are spoken in a school?

My parents came to the UK in the 60's as immigrants, though they had a language of their own, they always spoke to us, their children, in English as they wanted us to be able to assimilate into British/English society, when I went to Nigeria in 1981 I learnt to speak my language, Yoruba.

Personally, I have never met a non-White person who believes that Christmas or Easter should never be celebrated or that English should not be the language of instruction in Schools. If a child or adult cannot speak the language of the host country, then what chance do you have in becoming part of that society?

Children have an enormous capacity for picking up and learning new things, languages included. Agreed, some children may come to this country without being able to speak English, then extra support should be given to those children to help them to speak English. We shouldn't now say they have to be taught in whatever language it is they speak.

Come exam time, these children are not going to sit for their GCSEs writing Urdu, Polish, Latvian, Twi, Swahili, they will be required to write their exams in English. So why set them up with a disadvantage at the get go?

I am all for respecting and appreciating other cultures, however a certain amount of common sense needs to come into play, the goal must be to help people to assimilate not to remain separate.

My parents generation was one that placed such an emphasis on a British/English education with an emphasis on spoken English – how things have changed. Today, children are able to leave school without being able to write, read or even speak standard English, the expectations of teachers is almost zero, they are just happy to make it through the day without coming to any physical harm, add to that children who have been taught an admixture of English and several other languages in school, is it any wonder we are producing semi-illiterate school leavers?

During this time of economic recession it makes sense for the government to do away with all this wastage of money and ensure that English is the only spoken language in schools, unless of course a new language is being taught, such as French or German, etc. Why waste money on translation services, which in my view does not help people to learn the language. If someone requires help with translation, the onus should be on the individual to find a friend or family member to help with such.

During times of economic depression, people always look for a scapegoat to blame for their sorrows and woes and despite the fact that most Black people in this country are second or third generation born – some go back seven generations – because we stand out, we make easy and perfect targets.

I have often asked myself why we as Black people have failed to make it in the UK? Our history in the UK has not been as traumatic and barbaric as those of Black people in America, racism has played a part in us being held back but all cannot be blamed on racism, we as Black people must take some of the blame. Part of our problem is that we are not unified; I once read a book about how Asian people and British Asians had managed to do so well, irrespective of religion, i.e., Sikh, Hindu or Muslim, all pulled together.

Three friends might come together, pool their resources to buy a property for one friend and do the same until each member of the group became a property owner. Today, you can visit some areas and the entire area is predominately Asian or

Asian-British with the vast majority of them being property owners.

Unfortunately, we in the Black community do not seem to have this mindset, too many of us are too preoccupied with looking good and cool rather than helping one another out and carving out a name and a legitimate power base for ourselves.

Even when we set up a little business we all too often let ourselves down in the sense that friends and family now start flocking around and the smell of weed at times starts to permeate the surroundings. Customer service starts to go downhill and you the customer suddenly find yourself in competition with friends trying to get the attention of the owner whilst trying to make a payment for items purchased.

Business and friends do not mix, if you are setting up a business, you are there to make money and expand not to smoke weed and socialise (not all Black business are like this, but I have seen a few). Why is it that the majority of shops that sell Afro-Caribbean food and products are not run by Black people?

Go to any White-run business, even if they are not that keen on you, you will at least get good customer service because they know they are in business for one reason – to make money. Weed will not be smoked on the premises and you will not find able-bodied young men milling around on the premises.

Any Black business that is set up needs to appeal to more than just Black people and people staffing the business need to be able to speak standard English enabling them to have a broader appeal – not everyone wants to be addressed as 'bruv' or 'blood'. It's not a matter of being snobbish, it's a matter of being professional.

On paper, one could argue that America is a more racist place than the UK, however, the irony of it all is that in all walks of life you can find Black people who have done extremely well. You have Black Mayors of major cities, Black chiefs of police, Black four star generals in the army, the Navy and Air force also have high ranking officers, Black Supreme Court judges, the list goes on and on. Where are the equivalents in UK society? This is where I believe the subtle racism comes into play in UK society, there are many brilliant people of colour but all too often they are overlooked and frustrated out of their careers.

Today, in America, we have a Black President, a Black Attorney General, America has had a Black Surgeon General, a Black National Security Advisor, a Black Chairman of the Joint Chiefs of Staff to name but a few high ranking positions in the American Government/Cabinet. Even as a young child I can remember Andrew Young serving as the United States Ambassador to the United Nations. His Appointment just 12 years after the 1965 Voting Rights Act would have been monumental, however, as a young child I would have been oblivious to the impact of his appointment.

Will we ever have a Black Prime Minister or Joint Chief of Staff in the UK? As things currently stand, things look pretty bleak. I am all for people speaking well and properly, however, it seems that if one does not speak like the Queen, it is quite hard to progress in politics or the military. I am not sure if we even have any Black people above the rank of Colonel in any of the armed forces. Most of the high-ranking personnel seem to have a very cut glass accent and double-barrelled elongated surnames.

Can you imagine someone with a Liverpudlian or Mancunian accent rising to the position of Prime Minister or Attorney General in the UK? Throw in a bit of colour and the cards are really stacked against you. This is where subtle snobbery, elitism and racism creeps in where the UK is concerned.

I have a friend who has two degrees, one in History and one in Law; however, he has never been able to get into the legal profession. Most Black people that do eventually get into the legal profession, usually end up doing immigration law which has no real standing. Where are the Black lawyers working in corporate law, dealing with mergers and acquisitions?

We also see double standards at play with names, we are all aware of the so called 'ghetto names' like Shaniqua, Deshawn, Shaquanda etc. Chardonnay a few years ago was all the rave amongst a lot of White folk as a name to bestow upon their children. If we are going to judge or criticise strange names, we should judge also the strange names that are found in the White community, if not, live and let live.

We live in an age of equal opportunities, at least in the West, however, the ideal of equal opportunities to some extent has created more problems than solutions; by this, I mean in an attempt to create an all inclusive society. People who really should have no business in the public eye are elevated to celebrity status simply because they have the ability to be ignorant, obscene and crass and impressionable young people believe that by being uncouth, dense and uneducated they can become famous. While some people might be able to become famous by being like this, the road to destruction, incarceration and marginalization is littered with many who have adopted this way of life.

The entertainment industry is extremely savvy and by endorsing and elevating one or two of these so called urban individuals, they manage to kill two birds with one stone, i.e. the illusion is created that young Black youths with very limited education can become famous and also maintain the status quo, that Black people have to have lower standards to make it in the industry.

However many people have noted that in England many Black professionals or sports stars do not have Black partners, wives or girlfriends. I have heard many reasons put forward for this, some say that for Black men a White woman is the ultimate catch as the media is always promoting the White woman as the paragon of beauty, hence a White partner means they have the best thing going. Conversely, it is also claimed that a lot of White women see the Black man as the ultimate catch as well, as he is allegedly extremely gifted down below.

None of these assertions are true; unfortunately these myths have been propagated for years that they are now assumed to be truth.

One does have to ask ,why is it that many successful Black men do have a White partner? Is it that they have an aversion to Black women or is it that the path that has brought them success has not allowed them to meet Black women along the way? Personally speaking, you cannot help who you fall in love with and if love comes in the form of a White, Asian or Oriental woman so be it.

If Black women are marrying White men or vice versa, one doesn't really have to ask why, as such. For me, it is a good thing, for one, it shows that prejudice and racism are being challenged and conquered. You cannot say because you are Black you can therefore only date or marry someone who is Black. You marry or date the person who you believe is the most compatible for you, who is like minded and shares the same dreams and aspirations and values.

I have heard it said that a lot of Black women marry or date White men because of the element of financial security. If that is indeed true, that is quite a risk to take as we all know that money comes and money goes. If someone is rich today, there is no guarantee that in twenty years time they will still be wealthy.

It has also been said that a lot of Black men go for White women as Black women are too difficult or loud or angry. From my personal point of view, if I was a Black women and the initial deciding criteria for choosing a partner was ethnicity, i.e. choosing someone of the same race, then the person I would choose would be someone who is responsible, educated, well dressed and decent. Too many Black males (not all) seem to think that the Black experience consists of sagging jeans, limited responsibility and a truncated education. The Black experience is so much more diverse and more dynamic than that.

If a Black woman cannot find the qualities that she is looking for in a man in the Black community, then she should look elsewhere. We have to stop accepting mediocrity. The same applies to Black males.

Because of this emphasis of European/Caucasian beauty a lot of women have gone to drastic measures and have ultimately ended up disfiguring themselves. I have seen many Black women who have gone to bleach their skin in a bid to become lighter, some of these experiments have gone disastrously wrong and some of these women have ended up looking quite frightening. I remember coming across a few women in Nigeria who had bleached and in some of these cases, these women had a very strong smell (not pleasant), emanating from them.

Oriental and Asian women are just as bad, some of these women have done strange things to themselves with regards to bleaching and skin lightning and look quite hideous. Some of them actually look like they have been dead for a few years, they look totally lifeless and unreal. The best looking Asian and Oriental women that I have seen are those that look like Asian women and Oriental women should look like and not a poor imitation of White woman.

The irony of the whole situation is that while some women of colour are trying to get rid of their colour, White women are trying to add to their colour. Fake tans, sun beds and natural tans are now the vogue for a lot of White women as they complain that their natural colour leaves them looking lifeless.

What women of colour, especially Black women, are failing to understand is that they have beautiful skin, our skin retains its elasticity, hence the need for them to not have to inject fillers, etc. into their faces.

It is funny though, that no one seems to really make a song and dance about the desire and steps White women will take to stay youthful and beautiful by resorting to fake tans, sunbeds, plastic surgery etc.

Black women too have bought into the concept of European beauty, the hair industry alone in America is worth about two billion dollars a year if not more. Black women will attach, weave and glue the hair of Caucasian, Brazilian or Indian women to their own all in a bid to be 'beautiful'. If our hair was meant to be straight, long and wavy, I'm sure we would have been created that way, the creator would have made us that way, however, in his infinite wisdom he gave us lovely kinky hair as in our original home, it is hot and humid, and long, wavy hair and glue do not mix in thirty degree heat, especially when it is not washed for two to three months.

Imagine if the Black American weaned itself of its addiction to fake hair for just one year. That two billion dollars could be used so much more productively. There is nothing wrong in looking good, however our definition of beauty has become so narrow.

In many respects it is a hard battle to fight if not win, I remember back in the early 90s I too fell prey to the relaxing/ Jheri curl movement and why not, these were the images that

Black America if not America as a whole were projecting that cool and successful Black people looked like.

Today, the campaign is more aggressive and subtle, 'successful', 'beautiful' Black people are not really 'Black', they fluctuate from being honey coloured to butterscotch coloured. They have long wavy hair if you're a woman or short curly hair if you're a man (courtesy of sportin' waves) and your eye colour is hazel if you're lucky enough to have that as part of your genetic make up, if not, coloured contacts will suffice. Last but not least, that 'flared' nostril has to be nice and pointy. Beverley Hills' finest plastic surgeons can also help on that front.

Black people are all too eager to shout about their Cherokee, Creole, Indian, Irish bloodlines etc. but how many in the White community are eager to do the same? More often than not, if there is Black blood in the family, it is often something that is seen as a dark family secret and not talked about.

Don't get me wrong, I'm all for mixed relationships, my children are part Nigerian and Jamaican, my wife also has a part Chinese auntie, so on her side of the family there is a mix of all kinds as she herself is very light skinned and has green eyes. There just needs to be more of a balance between us as Black people ourselves and the media.

We only seem to have 'good hair' if our bloodlines are mixed. **WRONG,** our hair is good all the time, if I am 100% unadulterated Black, Negroid African, my hair is good. If I happen to have a little Mexican or European in me, my hair is still good. No hair is bad.

We really have to get this message, otherwise, what message are we passing to our kids, especially our daughters. They are only beautiful if their hair is long, wavy and permed? No other community sends out such destructive messages to its own people.

European women are beautiful with their long wavy hair, Black, African women are beautiful with their kinky hair, be it in braids, plaits, corn rolls or even with a number one cut. Why are we trying to be something that we were not created to be? Beauty is unique and the beauty of Black people is unique; some people will like it, some will not.

The idea or ideal of what is beauty or beautiful has so affected the Black community, until we can love ourselves for who we are and what we are, we will constantly feel inferior and buy into the concept of Western beauty.

In the past, light-skinned Black women made it into fashion magazines and of late we have seen a few dark-skinned Black women in these magazines, however, those of a darker hue just seem to be Black women with European features, high cheekbones, pointed nostrils. In some cases these 'Black' women are what some have termed to be "hybrid" women, half Black, half Latino or half Black, half Asian.

Beauty is universal; its starting point is not Europe, if it were a level playing field, why are we not making noise about the next supermodel who has been discovered, i.e., a white girl with Negroid features. Iman and Naomi Campbell are both beautiful women, but their beauty leans more towards a perception of what European beauty is.

How brainwashed, have we become that some of our people now need to bleach their skin in order to become lighter in complexion? Not only do these people have extremely low self-esteem, they will most likely end up being very lonely. Who will love a person that does not love themselves? To make matters worse, some men have now resorted to doing this, amongst Africans, it seems to be prevalent amongst men from the Congo and some Nigerian men amongst other Africans. Some of the men look ridiculous, apart from looking unnatural, their 'yellow' faces are now littered with Black spots, maybe from where the process has gone wrong or the effect of adolescent acne is now highlighted, reminiscent of a dessert we use to have at school as kids, called spotted dick.

What messages do these people pass down to their own children or loved ones? We as Black people have gone through enough without these poor representatives of our race adding to the burden we already carry.

Less than seventy years ago young Black males would be lynched for allegedly whistling at White women. Can you imagine Jews working to desecrate the memory of the Holocaust?

In his book, *All God's Children*, Fox Butterfield highlights some of the violence and terrorism directed towards Black people. He recounts an incident in 1890 when a White man had just taken delivery of a new pistol and emerging from the Post Office from where he had collected the pistol, he wanted to see if it worked. A shot was fired and a Black man was killed, no arrest was made, no inquest was held.

In another instance, mention is made of a young Black boy, who allegedly wrote an insulting letter to a White woman. At the court hearing, even though the boy was found to be illiterate, the young boy was found guilty and a light prison sentence was imposed. After the hearing, the head of the jury stated that they had to find him guilty so that his life could be saved. As unbelievable as this sounds, this was probably true, Butterfield states that in 1898 alone, as many as seventeen African-Americans were lynched.

The tragic shooting of Trayvon Martin in America shows that America still has a long way to go where race relations are concerned. Many Blacks felt that the shooting was due to his ethnicity, many Whites held a different opinion. What I found strange was that initially, the shooter was allowed to walk away freely. It only seemed to be after national and international interest that an arrest was made. I am not sure if a Black person shot someone and the police knew who they were, they would be allowed to walk away freely, I could be wrong, however, I just don't feel that would be the reality of things.

When America launched the war on terror, it would seem that this did not exempt African-American males living within the borders of the United States. Since 1619 the African-American male has been terrorised by those who view him as a threat and potential criminal.

I have read of about twenty cases where law enforcement officials have killed unarmed Black men in America. Some of the more well known cases are those of Amadou Diallo, Sean Bell and Oscar Grant. In almost every case, the so called law enforcement agent(s) have walked free without any charges being brought against them. For many the election of President Obama signalled a post-racial America, but in reality old habits die hard.

America needs to have a serious discussion about race, but on both sides, Black and White there is still so much anger, hatred and denial. The Truth And Reconciliation Commission in South Africa helped the country 'move on' from its ugly racial past, maybe something along the same lines needs to be implemented in America. Ignoring, isolating and demonising Black people in America will not make the issue of race disappear, it is a problem that needs to be exposed, confronted and dealt with.

Since the Trayvon shooting I have come across a few articles where fathers have sat down and spoken with their teenage sons about how to dress, talk and react when visiting certain areas i.e. predominantly White neighbourhoods. In many respects it is sad that fathers are having to have such conversations, but in some cases it is all too necessary.

Part of the problem that America has selling democracy is

that it isn't really a democratic nation, on paper the ideals are great but the reality for thirty million or so African-Americans is usually something different. How can democracy be sold when in turn it is not practised; schools, churches and communities are segregated.

Not wanting to become too political, I doubt if America has ever been a democracy. Democracy was preached from 1776 onwards and yet people of colour were held in chains and never viewed or treated as equals. In more recent times, this 'democracy' under the pretext of democracy has massacred hundreds of thousands in El Salvador, Honduras, Guatemala, Nicaragua. Vietnam, also is not a too distant memory. In almost every war or insurgency, you can usually find the fingerprint of Uncle Sam, whether directly or indirectly.

I came across a statistic which, if true, is quite frightening. It stated that the United States, out of it's 237 year existence, has been at war for 216 years

Where the UK is concerned, democracy is not always practised. Democracy is often described as a government of the people by the people for the people. If that were the case why did Tony Blair's government not listen when over a million people took to the streets asking that 'their' government not go to war in Iraq.

David Cameron's government fares no better. In 2013, it cannot be described as a government representative of the people; not a single ethnic minority is to be found in his cabinet. Rather, it is a government of White, mainly privileged men and women who most likely want to ensure that the status quo is maintained. It is never about democracy, it is always about big business – hence banks being bailed out by tax payers' money.

It is no wonder that an underclass has emerged, as even

though people are told to play by the rules and work hard and do the right thing, it is always found to be that the rules are always changing, for the rich at least and the laws that keep the rest of the populace in place do not apply for the rich and powerful. This sub class/under class will always continue to exist and in the main be made up of people of colour.

How does a child from an estate in Peckham or Brixton compete with a child from leafy Surrey whose parents have connections left right and centre and whose ancestry includes Dukes, Barons, Viscounts and Earls. The child from the inner city may have the same if not better educational qualifications, but the Old Boy network/White privilege will oftentimes be the overriding factor in favour of the White child.

Having said that, ethnic minorities should not be put off from the pursuit of education, as education is the most powerful of all things.

If indeed we have not imbibed the message to hate ourselves, would we be bleaching and destroying our skin? Why give preferential treatment to light-skinned Black people as Black people ourselves? Why is the so-called Black on Black violence we have today on both sides of the Atlantic? Young Black boys today in England killing themselves over a piece of land that they do not own, the turf or 'Ends' they are fighting for is land owned by someone other than themselves.

I have just come across a statistic, which, if indeed is true, is absolutely horrendous and terribly disturbing. Approximately 153 Black males are killed each week in America, 94% of them at the hands of another Black male. No source is given for this data, however, as stated, if indeed it is true it is a shocking waste of life, talent and development. How can things change if 7956 young men a year are dying unnecessarily. To put it in perspective America has lost approximately 6374 men and women fighting two wars in Iraq and Afghanistan from 2001-2012. In a time of peace almost 8000 men a year are dying and nothing is being done.

Black people in the main are killing themselves for land and property they do not own, turning their communities to battle zones and no-go areas, it doesn't get any more messed up than that, we really have taken the message to heart to hate ourselves.

Black women are torturing themselves and in some cases destroying themselves to attain something that they already have. No other race is as diverse as we are, from those who are charcoal Black to those who border on an almost vanilla complexion. We have enriched so many cultures and communities and yet are still unhappy with the origin or starting point of where all the beauty came/comes from. Black people have enriched Native American communities, European communities and even Asian communities.

In Japan there is a saying that to be a good samurai warrior, you need a bit of Black in recognition of early Black influences in Japan.

There needs to be a look back to the 60s/70s when Black was beautiful and we as Black people had a love of self. We weren't proclaiming to be better than others, we just acknowledged who we were and were comfortable and confident with that. We had uplifting songs like 'Young, Gifted and Black', not about bitches and ho's and shooting one another.

For centuries anything Black has been portrayed as bad, I am sure we can all reel off words and statements that portray Black as negative: Black sheep, Blacklisted, Black Mark, Black Market, Black Magic, Blackmail, Blackguard, etc. The only derogatory word that alludes to White that I can think of is White Elephant.

Two stories recently caught my eye on the BBC website

recently and I think both are pertinent to the state of race relations in the UK today. The first focused on GCHQ, one of the branches of British Intelligence, their job basically is to listen in on any and every form of communication within the UK.

GCHQ has a workforce of approximately 5000 officers, of the workforce 125 or 2.5% are Black or Asian, the majority of these 2.5% are employed as lower paid linguist or translator roles, only 1% are of junior or middle management grade.

Black and Asian Officers said they felt that they had to work twice as hard as their White counterparts for less pay, some even claimed to have heard comments like, "I didn't know we had people like that working here".

Is it any wonder that the war on terror is failing miserably? People who are British born and bred who have the knowledge and skills to help win this war are discriminated against when they offer their services to the land of their birth. I very much doubt that GCHQ are the only ones guilty of such blatant institutional racism, none of the armed forces really fares any better. Banks, the police, government and the judiciary are not much better either. Is it coincidental that Black and Brown faces are scarcely represented in these positions of power?

The second story I read focused on a Somalian family with seven children who, according to the report, were adequately housed, however, as they did not like the area they were living in, they complained to the local authority who now decided to re-house them in a £2m house in a very affluent part of London.

The report goes on to mention that the cost of rent to the taxpayer is £2000 a week. The father/husband is currently unemployed and is looking for work. I am not sure what job he will find that will enable him to pay £8000 a month towards his rent.

Most British/English people do not have a problem with genuine asylum seekers who need help, however how is someone meant to feel who has been waiting for a Council or Housing Association property for years when they see someone who has no affiliation to the country as such and is not working, living in a £2m house? If they were not racist before, such stupid actions by councils could turn them into racists.

If the family is adequately housed, why re-house them in a £2m house or if the need to re-house them was so dire, surely a £300,000 property would have been sufficient.

Callous and irresponsible gestures and policies like these help to polarise the different communities in the country, even I as an 'ethnic minority' feel outraged when I hear stories like these which seem to be all too frequent.

When people comment about these stories, they are suddenly branded racist, how can it be racist to comment about an action that is unfair and indefensible.

I use myself as a perfect example; my daughter who is severely disabled, has an inability to walk, talk and feed among other ailments, however, we as a family have been unable to get a Council property or Housing Association property despite having paid tax and national insurance for the last twenty one years. I am Black and British born and it makes me mad when people are suddenly housed in properties that I can only dream about. It is not racist to talk about these things and councils in my opinion should be fined for such irresponsible practices. By all means give help to those who need it, however, it cannot come at the cost of neglecting those who are citizens of the country, there needs to be a balance.

I'd like to also touch on the use of the N word. Many stupid, illiterate and ignorant people use this word as a greeting amongst themselves, their argument is that they are taking ownership of the word thus negating the impact of it. A lot of closet racist white people have also jumped on the band wagon saying that if Black people can use this word to greet and describe themselves, why can't they. What both these stupid, Black and White people do not realise is that it is only a certain group of Black people that use this word, can you imagine anyone who really understands the impact of racism or the struggle that Black people have gone through using this word?

Because a few dumb Black people use this word it does not mean that they now speak on behalf of every Black person or the Black community. Any White person that uses the above argument is either a closet racist or incredibly stupid, for Black people that use that term, they should have a rethink. The gay community does not use homophobic language when they meet and greet, why should we continue to denigrate ourselves and give ammunition to those who would also do the same.

The Black community need to rekindle that spirit of brotherhood. How is it that we have managed to lose it in a generation? Back in the 60's when we referred to each other as brother or sister it meant something and we would have acted as such, today those terms are just used to try and sound cool.

Recently, my brother-in-law, who happens to be White, and I went out to buy a pair of shoes for his son, my nephew and we arrived at the shopping mall. As we were about to enter the complex we passed by a Black man and we both exchanged greetings by way of a nod of the head. Though no words were exchanged the nod of the head was profound in the sense that we both acknowledged that we were the only Black faces around, almost as if to say that if anything happens I've got your back or that it was refreshing to see another Black face in a predominately and extremely White environment.

I have gone through the encounter in my mind a few times and it just brings a smile to my face, on the other hand it has made me think how hard and difficult it is for the non-ghetto or street Black man. He has to deal with racism and also the threat of street and ghetto Black men who think he is not 'Black' enough and who also want to make his life hell. What a burden to carry.

How is the problem of inequality to be addressed, especially in England? Mike Fuller the former Chief constable of the Kent police force (the only "ethnic minority" to attain such a position within the police force) felt that Black officers have to work twice as hard as their White colleagues to get promoted. Even in his case that would be said to be true, he has a number of degrees, across the UK, no other Chief Constable has as many qualifications and degrees as him. Why is that?

In America, affirmative action programmes have helped many people of colour to become fully integrated into American society on all levels. Although it has its detractors I believe that affirmative action has its place as a useful tool as long as it is employed properly, I don't believe you should just put a person in a position simply because they are Black, however, I do believe that if a Black person has potential and is educationally qualified, he or she should be given a helping hand. An example could be if a certain position were to be filled and two candidates, both Black and White have the same score and there was a scarcity of both Black and Brown faces in that particular position, the non-white candidate should get the job.

Also, with affirmative action, I believe that timescales should be introduced, i.e. a five year window, otherwise, the purpose would be defeated. Affirmative action should never be about lowering standards, it should be about creating a level playing field.

I have not always held this view, however, when I look back

on the history of Black people, especially in America I think it is a good thing. I believe that to an extent we have forgotten the journey that the Black man has had to make in America. He was taken to a foreign land in chains, denied any form of justice, denied education, constantly kept subjugated, he could be discarded like a broken toy if his master so desired. Even when working the sugar cane fields, some slaves had their mouths padlocked so as to not eat into the profits of the master.

If the master wanted to have sex, he could take the wife of the slave as both were his property and did not have any rights; in fact they were not even deemed to be humans. Any dissent from the slaves was dealt with ruthlessly and resulted in severe floggings and many times killings by the master.

When a people have been denied education, freedom, dignity respect, employment, health care, good housing etc. for centuries, how can they contribute effectively to society. Yes, slavery ended many years ago, but the legacy it left behind hasn't.

Today many Black children in America start life from a disadvantaged standpoint from White children, their schools receive less funding; the school buildings are in a state of decline. The neighbourhoods they grow up in are run down and have higher crime rates than White neighbourhoods.

Not knowing the history and struggle of Black people it becomes all too easy to say "why can't Black people get their act together and just get on with it" – probably we could if we had a level playing field but so far that has not been the case.

Take Lloyds or JP Morgan, they have been around for centuries, what companies or organisations do Black people have that have been around for this length of time? Whilst these organisations were busy making money probably directly or indirectly from the toil and sweat of Black people, Black people were still in the fields picking cotton and sugar cane for the White man, his children were being breast fed by Black nannies and beautiful mansions were being built for him to live in by the same Black men who were deemed to be brutish beasts.

If a people or a group has an economic, political and educational head start of three hundred years or more against another then it becomes difficult for the disadvantaged group to close the gap as quickly as it would like especially when obstacles and barriers are continually placed in their path.

As I have mentioned earlier, the media is a very powerful tool, this was brought home to me in 2005 when Hurricane Katrina battered the Southern coast of the United States, the images that were beamed into peoples houses around the world showed a picture that America has tried to hide. One of neglected, and forgotten communities. If it wasn't for the fact that we had been told that this disaster had taken place in America, viewers could easily have thought this natural disaster was taking place in Africa, the images we saw in the main were of poor, wretched and bedraggled Black people.

Normally this would not be a picture that America would want the world to see, when America is usually shown in the news or films, we see the beautiful images of New York, Las Vegas, Beverly Hills and the like. America is not the only country guilty of such selective broadcasting; the UK is just as guilty.

As with the media, image and perception are also equally as important in forming impressions and opinions of what the 'truth' or 'norm' is. For instance, if people were asked to visually describe what a South African, Australian or American looked like, the majority would most likely describe someone who was Caucasian, despite the fact that people of colour have lived in these countries for centuries and in some cases, before Caucasians arrived. Generally speaking, the images of what these people should look like or what the media believe these people should look like is what the media thrusts upon us.

The saying 'As American as apple pie' comes to mind. Why does apple pie have to be the barometer for gauging American culture? If it is at all possible to capture the fullness of the American experience in one sentence. Why not 'As American as grits or bagels' or 'soul food'?

When Africa is shown in the news, all we ever seem to see are images of war and famine, if we are lucky we might be shown images of a safari.

Africa does have numerous problems like any other country or continent, but there are also some beautiful places in Africa in terms of scenery, architecture etc. Why are these places never shown? I suppose it is to someone's benefit to still portray Africa as the Dark Continent and not the birth place of civilization.

I mentioned earlier that I have always found it easier to identify and describe myself as a Nigerian, however over the last twenty or twenty five years a strange dynamic has taken place. When I was younger and introduced myself to people, i.e. told them my name, the next question was usually, where are you from or where does that name originate from. Now it is totally different, if I introduce myself to people, they are now the ones to usually say, "that's a Nigerian name."

What has happened in those last twenty-twenty five years? Being Nigerian has now become synonymous with being a drug pusher or a '419' con artist.

170 million Nigerians are now labelled, tagged and stereotyped as being criminals or potential criminals. Imagine if we were to label every German as a Nazi or every White American as a racist or a serial killer, I am sure there would be uproar and rightly so. However, it seems to be okay to lump every single Nigerian into a box.

I remember some years ago it was said that a certain airline and a certain bank were refusing to take credit card payments from Nigerians who wished to purchase Airline tickets. The bank was also allegedly refusing to open bank accounts as they were both afraid of being scammed. Imagine if Nigeria refused to let any unaccompanied white male into the country as he is deemed to be a potential pervert/child molester. Would it be so bad, as Nigeria would just be applying the same logic as the majority of paedophiles in the UK are White, therefore, every White male is a paedophile or has a proclivity to be a paedophile.

Rather than tar an entire nation, try and deal with each individual as they present themselves

African-American actors have made great strides in America unlike here in the UK, the funny thing here in the UK is that many times if a film is shown on TV that has a predominately Black cast, such a film or programme will not usually be shown at prime time, anytime after 11pm is usually the norm.

Black British actors normally struggle to get any decent roles here in the UK and to really flourish in their trade, they are usually left with no other option than to go to America and break the trend of being cast as thugs, pimps, hookers and crack heads.

Back to the issue of the press. Can you imagine how things would have been reported if the current economic meltdown we are facing was due to the fact that Black people were in charge of the world economy? I can just imagine some of the comments: "you know what those Black people are like" , "you can never trust a Black man to run things". The people that have put us in the mess we are in are rightly condemned, but their race never comes into play, if the shoe was on the other foot I don't think we would be afforded the same luxury without our race also being made mention of. Irrespective of colour there are greedy people everywhere.

When President Obama was elected to the White House, there was a massive fanfare as "change" had finally come to America, (well at least on the political landscape anyway.) Now that the honeymoon period has somewhat worn off, President Obama's ratings are quite low, but what has Obama done that is so wrong, he has introduced healthcare for a lot of people that look like him and that evidently has got the backs up of a large majority of people that do not look like him.

After over two hundred years of White men running a country that is not really theirs, someone whose people (Africans) have contributed a lot to the country starts running the show and suddenly there is a hue and cry. A similar situation is occurring in South Africa and I guess the same would probably happen if an Aboriginal Australian was lucky enough to be able to govern the country.

I have often wondered if there really is any advantage for Black people being born in the West and at the moment I have to say that I believe it to be a disadvantage. Our kids grow up with no real sense of identity, if they are of African origin, most of them cannot speak their language, they are blissfully unaware of their history, culture, heritage. Now that education seems to have taken a back seat, most grow up being unable to read, write or speak English properly. Ghetto life and street life are dragging our kids into a spiral of death, violence and imprisonment.

Our liberal and hands off society allows for everything so that when our kids, those that are lucky to, grow up and attend interviews for work, they have no interview techniques or skills, are unable to pick up on non-verbal cues and hints and then get disillusioned when they cannot find employment.

If you look like a thug, walk like one leg is longer than the other and grab your crotch, don't be surprised if you don't get a job.

We have been brainwashed and led to believe that in Britain there is a freedom to be who you want. A lot of Black people now look like cartoon characters covered from head to toe with tattoos, men and boys are corn rolling their hair (nothing wrong with corn rolls as long as they are well maintained), people are getting grills (rows of gold teeth) and think they are super cool. Some of our women have outrageous and strange hair styles, have no decorum in their mode of dressing and then wonder why only White people have the good jobs.

In general, the top lawyers, barristers, bankers, academics and other professionals are White.

They understand that from an early age, discipline, self respect, speaking properly and dressing properly all have an advantage and play a powerful role for later life, we as Black people need to learn this lesson fast.

What's the point of sending your kids to school in the latest trainers with an iPod blaring out music only for your child to leave school with no qualifications, social skills or common sense?

As mentioned earlier, great strides have been made in Race Relations in Britain, however, there are still far too many Black people (suitably qualified) that are under-employed or not employed simply because of their colour.

You can hide your sexuality, but you cannot hide your colour.

If Africa had good governance, is there any real reason for Black people to be in Britain? We have fresh food back home, not pumped full of additives, preservatives, E numbers and the like, we have culture, traditions, languages, we have an appreciation of our elders and the knowledge and wisdom that most of them have. Our weather is beautiful; the extended family structure is far more beneficial that the nuclear family set up.

Why are we so quick to abandon everything from our history to our language? What has the West imbibed from Africa? We have taken on their legal system, language, mode of dressing, religion, customs etc. yet with our aping of everything Western, where has it taken us? I am not saying everything Western is bad, however, not everything Western is good either.

I remember contracting malaria several times in Nigeria, at times, rather than take the ubiquitous chloroquine that often made me itch and scratch, I would sometimes opt for traditional methods of cure such as drinking the liquid of leaves or bark that had been infused in water. These cures have been tried and tested and Western medicine has found them to be not wanting, however as these cures do not come in pretty packages, the West and a number of us as Africans believe them to be primitive.

The case of two gay men in Malawi made me smile, initially they were sentenced to fourteen years in jail, however after pressure from aid agencies and a famous American female singer the pair were spared time in prison. When the case first came to light, people said how barbaric and backward Malawi was. What many failed to mention or chose to ignore is that the law the couple were sentenced under is the same law that the British introduced, as they did in many parts of Africa.

The same applies to religion, Europeans introduced Christianity to Africa, now that God has gone out of vogue in Europe and the West, Africans that have held on to Christianity are now seen as deluded or lacking some sort of mental capacity or capability.

Before Europeans came to Africa, Africans had their own laws and religion and their societies were well run and orderly, we were not eating each other and running around naked, as a lot of biased and bigoted films and books would have you believe.

I get quite upset with the way that we as Africans are so quick to abandon our culture, history and heritage for something that we can never have – someone else's culture. I remember when I was in Nigeria and you would come across people who had never even left Lagos let alone the country speaking with a terrible phoney American accent. Why try and be something you are not, the best person you can be is yourself. If you are born abroad fine, then you will have a different accent, however, if you have never set foot on a plane how is your accent going to be like that of a New Yorker?

Many African communities are crumbling because we as Africans have forgotten who we are and are trying to be something that we are not. I think we can learn something from the Asian (Indian) community here in the UK, they have held on to their culture and traditions and yet can be British or English when the occasion requires.

I think that if we held on to some of the things in our culture, family, respect and hard work then some of the issues that currently bedevil the Black community would be diminished.

It is great that America has elected its first African-American President, but the issue of race will always rear its ugly head.

On one hand if President Obama does a sterling job, he will not be viewed as an African-American, he will be viewed as a mixed race or bi-racial President and those with an agenda will be quick to point to his Caucasian bloodline as being the reason that he was able to do such a good job.

On the other hand if he does a terrible job, he will definitely be referred to as the first Black President by the mainly White majority.

Recently there was a bit of a hoo-hah in one of the papers, the *Metro*, about Black History Month. A reader had written in to complain about the Black community having a whole month dedicated to it, the reader felt that this in itself was racist. The following day, another reader wrote in and said why should there be a complaint about Black History Month as for eleven months of the year; everything else is about the White community.

In many respects I agree with the latter, for eleven months of the year, the focus is on the predominant group which is the White community and rightly so, the only time when Black people seem to get any attention, well at least as far as the press is concerned, is when there are shootings and stabbings.

It seems that we cannot win, when we celebrate Black History Month and showcase the contributions that Black people have made over the hundreds of years they have been here there is a big fuss, when Black people make the news for gun and knife crime, there is a fuss.

Adoption is another area where race seems to show its ugly side, many Brown and Black children adopted in the 50s and 60s went through terrible times in the UK. Great strides have been made since then, however, the default position again always seemed to be White families adopting Black children. More often than not, these children went into good homes, but oftentimes, these children were left with an identity crisis – they spoke like White people, took on their "culture" but were not white, they looked like Black people, but in most cases knew nothing about "Black culture" and had probably never met Black people themselves.

What I have never seen, even though attitudes have greatly changed since those days is a Black family with a White adopted child. If White parents can be deemed to provide a loving, nurturing and suitable home for Black children, why cannot the same be true in the reverse. There may be such families out there, however, I have not had the privilege of meeting them and when I say the privilege, I do not use the word in a sarcastic or insulting manner.

It almost appears to be the case that Black families are "incapable"of providing suitable homes for White children in need of a home.

The recent spate of celebrity adoptions would seem to reinforce that position. I don't doubt that these celebrities mean well, however, the picture or message that seems to come out again is that these children's lives can only be bettered if they are removed from their cultures and countries and go and live with a wealthy White benefactor. Money is not an issue for these celebrities, what might have been better is if they had set up trust funds for these orphans and let them be raised by well to do/Black middle-class families in their country of origin. That way, the children get the material benefit that money can buy and still get to retain their cultural identity.

Football is another area where race plays a big role, I have often wondered where all the Black faces are on match day in the crowd.

Back in the 70s and early 80s professional Black football players suffered terrible racist abuse from a mainly White intolerant and ignorant crowd. Back then it was a brave person of colour that went to a football match.

Today, things are vastly improved; very rarely will you hear racist abuse coming from the crowd. Unfortunately, things are not quite the same in Eastern Europe where many of these countries are about fifty years behind Western societies when it comes to race relations. Black players are still subjected to vile and unimaginable racist abuse.

UEFA and FIFA, the governing bodies of football have been incredibly weak and slow to punish the countries where these bigots have been given free rein to carry on with impunity.

To some extent, I think Black people are still somewhat scarred by their experiences of the 70s and 80s hence the dearth of Black faces in the crowds.

If things were to get violent, what chance have you as a Black man against fifty White guys who have got a belly full of beer and suddenly wish they were living in 1970? Also what do you do as a Black father who takes his son to the football ground and suddenly encounters twenty guys who want to verbally abuse you in front of your son? It's easier to stay at home and watch the game on Sky TV.

Recently the Metropolitan Police claimed that it is investigating about twenty officers due to allegations of racism. At present the officers in question have been suspended. In many respects the Met finds itself in a very difficult situation. One of the officers who has been suspended has been caught on tape racially abusing a suspect and boasting of strangling him. With that case I have no problem at all as he clearly over-stepped the mark. I am not aware of the ins and outs of the other cases, however, the Met finds itself in the position of being damned if it acts and damned if it doesn't.

A lot of the problems the Met faces with regards to racism and allegations of racism could have been resolved a long time ago in the sense that it has been slow to act and change. Racism and allegations of racism have plagued the Met since the 60s, since people of colour first came to the UK in significant numbers. If the Met had not allowed racism to thrive and stamped it out amongst its ranks there and then, the problems we now have would not have been allowed to take root. Fifty years later we are still debating the same issue, which really is unacceptable.

I will concede that they do a challenging job under very trying circumstances, some have said that some of the officers used racist language whilst under pressure during the London riots. I don't buy that argument, I can accept an officer maybe using excessive force or very colourful language, but why does race have to come into it?

A friend once said to me that White people are racist and Black people are prejudiced, to agree with the statement would be unfair, ignorant and biased, however, there is an element of truth to what he said. Since making contact with Black people, White (not all) described Black people as monkeys, sub-human and primitive. Black people were then forcibly removed from their homes and enslaved, they were murdered, raped and tortured for very minor infractions. They were denied the right to vote. Laws were introduced to prevent Blacks from marrying Whites. In South Africa, Blacks could only be in certain areas at certain times of the day and always had to carry some form of ID.

While in South Africa in 1997 I was arrested and thrown in Prison for a few hours as I had just gone across the road to a fast food restaurant to buy lunch and forgotten to take my passport with me. I doubt if many White people were stopped and detained in South Africa in those days. (I was in South Africa at the time with all the legitimate paperwork doing missionary work in case you wondered.)

Back to the above statement about White people being racist and Black people being prejudiced, I recently heard another argument put forward for the assertion. The writer said Black people could not be racist because they do not have the economic, political or judicial ability to be so. His argument was that racism was more than just a hatred of someone for being different, it was an ability to use power or processes of the state to hold back or deny certain people, usually those of a different colour from reaching their potential.

It certainly helps to see/show racism in a different light. I cannot say I am in agreement with the statement, but I can certainly see what he meant. If one looks at any country where there is a mix of Black and White people, generally speaking, the White minority or majority will usually have the economic and political clout and all other trappings of power

I could be wrong, however if we reverse the roles, I cannot see Black people doing the same or having done the same to White people. It could be argued that Robert Mugabe is doing something of the above in Zimbabwe, however, to a certain extent, I don't think his actions are driven by racism per se, his actions seem to be those of a man desperate to cling on to power by all means.

Oftentimes some White people are too quick to say that Black people are racist or are playing the race card and in some cases they would be right to say so, however, they are quick to forget that Black people have had to put up with inequality for four hundred years. When steps are taken to address the imbalances and inequalities that exist, some White people are quick to say that Black people are getting all the benefits, jobs and they are now the subject of racism. I would say to them, please read extensively about how Black people got to the Americas and UK, read up on laws that allowed for murders and lynchings to take place, research into how Black people were disenfranchised and denied the opportunity to vote. Read about slaves who were able to save up and buy their freedom only to lose their freedom and be re-enslaved again.

Luckily a lot of the above practices and policies have been done away with, however, the legacy still lives on in some of the stereotypes we have today of Black people and the way that certain people view Black people today.

How have stereotypes for Black people being able to survive for so long, the manual labour of African-Americans built America, but Blacks were seen as being lazy and hyper sexual. For one, many so-called enlightened men and women with letters after their names wrote books and journals based on so-called scientific knowledge to justify their bigotry and narrow-mindedness. Written and documented 'facts' are often hard to disprove even when supporting evidence comes to light to prove otherwise.

Black people have also inadvertently played into the hands of racial stereotyping, Blacks were/are seen as promiscuous and hyper sexual, the music videos that we see today, unfortunately reinforce that stereotype, however, Blacks in America have a history of having their families destroyed and torn apart – a father, daughter or mother could be sold at any time ripping apart a family that was already in place. Real relationships and lasting relationships could not be forged, a family member could disappear, die due to working conditions or be sold at any time. This does not excuse the state of many African-American families today, but it plays a part as people tend to copy what they have witnessed. Just as children who have been abused by their parents are more likely to abuse their own children. Children whose parents have struggled with alcohol or drug issues are more likely to struggle with the same once they attain adulthood.

Recently, I met with three friends, we had all previously worked together but have since left the organisation that we worked for. We usually meet once or twice a year for a pizza and just to catch up. We are quite a motley crew (to the untrained eye, no discernible difference would be found), however as I said we are quite a mixed bag; a Nigerian, a Jamaican, a Congolese and an Ethiopian. After a while we found ourselves talking about the state of Black relationships and violence not only in the Black community but also violence perpetrated by Black people in general.

Interestingly enough, I had also had the same conversation with another friend about two weeks prior to my reunion with the friends above, my friend also of Jamaican origin had a interesting take on things. He saw it as being a legacy of the slave trade in the sense that according to him, the most unruly and bellicose slaves were sent to Jamaica. Once they arrived in Jamaica, they were again subjected to the most shocking and appalling violence, evil and wickedness. According to him, a lot of the violence in Jamaica today can be attributed to its history. He cited two examples that were recorded in a newspaper that he had read recently.

One story was about a father and son who got in to an altercation about the last remaining piece of fish from their meal which resulted in tragic circumstances, i.e the death of one of the parties (I can't remember if it was the father or son, however, someone died). The other was about a British National who had Jamaican heritage and had gone to Jamaica, a disagreement arose regarding a phone charger and it appears that she was killed by a mob over the charger.

The three friends with whom I met all had their opinions as to the state of things in the Black community. When I mentioned what my other friend had said about Jamaica's slave legacy, the other Jamaican also agreed with me, he went further to say that a lot of the gun violence we have started with the Jamaicans and that African kids have now jumped on the band wagon.

He also mentioned how we have all been so brainwashed and how from generation to generation anger, hatred and self loathing is passed on. He spoke of his own upbringing, how his own mother would say that his hair was hard and coarse like peppercorn and how he needed to strengthen his nose. (I am not sure how you strengthen your nose.) As a Black African, my hair is meant to be tight, coarse, kinky, woolly or whatever term you want to use to describe it. My nose is meant to be flat, flared or broad, these are some of the distinguishing traits and characteristics that I have as a Black man.

He also mentioned how he had a dark-skinned friend, who was going out with a light-skinned Black girl and his mother's comment was to say, how did he manage to get her. A sad indictment of a lot of Black people's thinking that light skin equates to beauty. Nothing could be further from the truth, I have seen some stunningly and traffic-stopping amazingly beautiful ebony, mahogany looking women. Unfortunately, we don't celebrate that enough in the Black community, we pander to a poor imitation of Caucasian beauty.

Our so-called celebrities don't help matters any further by going under the knife to have their noses remodelled or reshaped to look like that of Caucasians or lightning or bleaching their skin. We are not White people and never will be, despite whatever drastic or radical procedures or operations we undergo. We are Black people, if you happen to have European features with that beautiful Black skin, great, if you don't, don't worry as you were not created to look like a European. We see images of Jesus depicted with blonde hair and blue eyes, but anyone with three or four brain cells knows that it is a total misrepresentation. Jesus would look more like anyone from the Middle East.

Fela Kuti, the multi-talented and Africa conscious musician married 27 women on one day, he referred to his wives as his Queens and rightly so, they were devastatingly beautiful Black women. I am not advocating polygamy, being from a polygamous home myself i.e. my dad has two wives, it might work if practised in the right manner (what that manner is, don't ask me as I don't know) but it appears to have worked in times gone by, today it has been corrupted and men use it more as a means to prove that they are still virile other than anything else.

The Western ideal of monogamy doesn't seem to be working out too well either, with one in two marriages not lasting the distance, and those that do stay together, oftentimes being a mere arrangement for the sake of the children, rather than being an active, loving and functioning relationship between husband and wife. On top of that, a lot of people are having or have had affairs, so maybe the Western model isn't so great after all. The traditional Mormons and Muslims could be on to something in terms of where marriage is concerned, who knows.

Going back to my earlier point, many so-called enlightened men and women have contributed to how Black people were/are perceived. In her book, *Medical Apartheid* Harriet Washington discusses how in the 1850s a Dr Samuel A. Cartwright. M.D. had published in medical journals how Blacks suffered from a host of imaginary illnesses and ailments. Dysthesia Aethiopic: a desire to destroy the property of White slave owners. Cachexia Africana was another illness which purportedly was exclusive to African-Americans and resulted in their eating non-edible food items. Today this is known as Pica, an ailment that crosses all racial boundaries.

African-Americans were used as guinea pigs for all kinds of horrendous and sadistic experiments all in the name of medical science. The Tuskegee syphilis experiment of 1932 is a scar on the conscience of America. The experiment consisted of six hundred African-American men being deliberately infected with syphilis and having treatment being withheld so that doctors could see the effect that the disease would have on people and a government cover up.

Blacks have also being used as guinea pigs with regards to being injected with radioactive substances, lobotomies have been carried out, prisoners have been used to try out substances and medicines that have not been approved and a litany of unspeakable crimes and horrors have been performed upon African-Americans all in the name of medical research and science. You cannot dehumanise a group of people and expect that such crimes will never see the light of day and not have consequences. For too long Black people have been labelled as savages, however, the treatment that has been meted out to Black people by some White people is barbaric and truly inhumane.

Sporting events can be occasions where racism again rears its ugly head, the 1936 Olympics in Berlin was meant to be a showcase of Hitler's Aryan supremacy, however Jesse Owens had different plans and was able to put that theory to rest by winning four gold medals.

I am not really a follower of American sports as such, but I can still remember when it was almost the norm to imply that African-Americans were not smart enough to play as quarterbacks in the American NFL and today the number of Black quarterbacks in the NFL is still very low.

In many respects, until quite recently, Black athletes were caught up in a no win situation where sports were concerned. If you were good at athletics people would say, it was to be expected as we ran barefoot all over the place and chased after animals. God help you if you happened to show any skill in the javelin, automatically, you would be labelled a "spear chucker".

Alternatively, if you showed no sporting prowess, again, you would fit the same stereotype, as being Black, how could you be good at anything as we were all deemed to be lazy.

The London Olympics of 2012 was a spectacular event, not just with regards to the medals British athletes won, but also with regards to the opening and closing ceremonies.

It really was an occasion when all Londoners and the rest of the UK came together, however, unfortunately, not all of the UK was behind the event, a conservative MP, described the opening ceremony as "Leftie multi-cultural crap", partly in reference to the well represented number of Black and Brown faces which showed/shows a true picture of how London is.

He obviously, does not/did not like the London of 2012. The local authority which he represents as a member of Parliament, Cannock Chase, based on estimates from 2011, has a population of 97,500. The latest figures that I could find for the population breakdown by ethnicity are as follows: White British, 94.39% Mixed race, 1.06% Asian or Asian British, 2.01% Black or Black British 0.53% Chinese, 0.21%.

If this particular MP lived in an inner London Borough, for example Lewisham or Brent where there are a lot of non-white faces (a lot, not the majority), then maybe he could argue that there were concerns that his constituency was being "swamped", to borrow a term used by Margaret Thatcher, the first female and Conservative British Prime Minister, but that is not the case.

I believe the MP was showing his true colours, the opening ceremony proved to be a little too "colourful" for him as it was a far cry from the comfort of his 94.39% White British constituency.

I am not sure if racism will ever be eradicated, however, we as Black people can play our part by not conforming to some of the stereotypes that some have of Black people.

CHAPTER FIVE

Drugs have done untold damage to the Black community, however, across the board we continue to deceive ourselves and wander around in a fog of ignorance and denial as to the cost of drug use and dependency of our people.

To some extent, we are lucky in the sense that drug use and damage has not reached the scale of that of America, but with time if drastic measures are not taken we will soon catch up with America.

Already, we hear of shootings in the Black community which we are told is often gang related or drug related, but who are the major players in the drug trade? Yes, we have the Jamaican Yardies, but there are other major if not bigger players than the Yardies. The Chinese Triads and Turkish criminals are major players in the drugs trade in the UK, but not much is really heard or mentioned about them.

Where drugs are concerned the Black community has a bad reputation more than most other racial groups, however, where drug consumption is concerned within the US, African-Americans are pretty much on par with other racial groups where drug usage is concerned. The portrayal of African-Americans and Blacks in general in films and the media would have us believe otherwise – that people of colour are responsible for all the drug wars, trade and usage in the world.

Here in the UK, the picture is pretty similar. However, when I Googled drug barons in the UK, my search revealed that all the drug barons were White, however, if you were to speak to the average man or woman on the street, the common misconception would again be that all the drug problems are the fault of the Black community.

The problem again is down to representation, for instance a White film star, actor or singer who is a known drug user will be described as a bit of a wild child and feted as a bit of a "jack the lad", however, if it were a Black person, I am sure the language used to describe them would be somewhat stronger.

We often read about certain celebrities who have a well known drug habit however, their "celebrity" status seems to keep them immune from prosecution for drug usage or possession, again I don't think any Black "celebrity" would be shown that same leniency if they were caught time after time in possession or usage of drugs.

We also hear about drug usage going on amongst corporate and city workers who tend to be White and the after dinner usage of coke (not the liquid kind) amongst White, middle-class professionals, but this does not seem to be an issue as they claim that no one is getting hurt and that they can give up any time as they are not addicts but recreational users – both assertions are rubbish. We in the Black community don't have the luxury about being so blasé about drugs and to some extent have deceived ourselves that drugs are not an issue within our community.

In the UK marijuana usage is quite widespread within the Black community and a number of our people are involved in the dealing of marijuana to earn a little extra on the side or in some cases as a full time occupation.

To date I have not really heard a genuine reason for marijuana usage, some say that it helps them to relax. If you want to relax then meditate or take a day off work or do something that you enjoy doing, apart from smoking weed.

Rather than learning a trade or staying in school too many

of our youths are busy just standing on street corners selling weed and not doing anything productive with their lives. Is their vision so stunted that all they can dream of becoming is a dope dealer?

A lot of arguments are put forward for Black youth turning to weed and I'm not really sure I buy the arguments, such as kids not having anything to do. Maybe because I'm from an African background, but I just could not ever give that as an argument to my father that I had nothing to do, therefore I turned to crime or petty dope dealing. Firstly, my father would say, "what do you mean, you have nothing to do, don't you have any books you can read?" and that would be the end of that conversation. Likewise, if I was standing idly around my Dad would always find something for me to do, so rather than be press ganged into doing some chores around the house, I would find a book to bury my head in.

Again for us as Africans, there is no such thing as the Welfare state, if you don't study and make something of yourself academically or by way of learning a trade, you will go hungry and if you steal from someone, unlike the UK justice system which literally nowadays rewards you for being a miscreant/felon, you will be burned alive on the streets of Lagos.

I think we have also forgotten what it means to have shame, as Africans if we have a dope smoker in the family, everyone will look down on you and you more than likely become an outcast, unlike here in the UK if you don't go out drinking every Friday and drinking yourself in to a state of catatonia or smoking dope, you are almost looked upon as though it is you that has the problem.

Marijuana usage is now looked upon as more of a social pastime rather than drug usage so it is not such a "big deal" if you smoke marijuana.

I remember a story a few years ago in the press where it was reported that Prince Harry was rumoured to be a marijuana user, it was interesting to see the response of Prince Charles. It was reported that Prince Charles took Prince Harry to a centre for recovering drug addicts so that he could get to see the reality of what drug usage and dependency really does.

I would like to think that a lot of parents in the Black community would do the same, however, I am not sure that many would, I hope I am wrong though.

Marijuana, like nicotine usage, has its effects. I am baffled as to why people would want to play Russian roulette with their health. Will every marijuana user move on to harder drugs or suffer from mental health issues? Probably not. Will every smoker suffer from cancer or emphysema? Probably not. However, the effects of cannabis usage on young Black people can be seen quite easily, one only has to take a trip to the Maudsley Hospital in South London to see the lives that have been wasted due to marijuana usage and addiction.

I think part of the problem for drug usage in the West is that we are too arrogant to learn from others, we tend to believe that everything Western is the best and therefore we cannot learn from others. My personal belief is that we are too soft on people who are drug addicts in this country, we are too quick to give excuses as to why people become hooked on drugs, we have all been through hard times, myself included, however, many of us do not resort to drugs for comfort or solace.

Many drug users are let off with a caution or verbal warning, I have yet to meet anyone who has given up their drug usage because of a verbal warning. Prison may not always be the best option, however, when we talk of community service, where are these people? Recently, we have had snow that has literally brought most parts of the country to a standstill; a lot of these people could have been drafted in to clear the snow that made most of the roads impassable.

My thinking may be a bit radical and drastic; however, what are the alternatives to act as a deterrent for drug usage? We have become so liberal now that we don't expect people to take responsibility for any of their actions and when their actions cause harm or injury to themselves or others, we are still too afraid to say that their actions have brought them to the predicament that they find themselves in.

We have this almost romanticised view of drugs in the UK. Recently I was speaking with someone and she was saying that when she was in Jamaica she felt chilled out as she was able to smoke her dope, I had to remind her that the smoking of weed in Jamaica is illegal (at present) and that if she was caught, there could have been serious consequences for her. Maybe a few nights in a Jamaican prison might have awoken her from her romantic reverie.

Drugs may grant temporary respite from the everyday difficulties that life presents, however, the long term "benefits" are usually not that beneficial. As far as drugs and Black people are concerned, we can do better.

CHAPTER SIX

R ace and crime are extremely contentious issues and depending on which side of the fence you sit on, you may believe that Black people are responsible for every criminal activity known to man or that Black people just like White people commit their own fair share of crime.

Having said that, in some inner cities Black people are over-represented in some areas of crime, more than any other ethnic groups.

We can shout racism till the cows come home, however, in London the majority of gun and knife crime is committed by Black males.

Some conspiracy theorists say that Black people do not make guns and that somehow others have a hand or are really behind all the gun crime in the Black community, it is true that Black people do not make guns, however, it is not White people that are shooting Black people, it is Black people most of the time knifing and shooting one another, hence the term in the UK "Black on Black" crime.

I cannot say that I am entirely comfortable with the term Black on Black crime. Are we saying that in some ways that the crimes that Black people commit are somehow different to crimes committed by other racial groups? White people and Asian people commit the same crimes as Black people – robberies, rapes, murders etc. A lot of White people are involved in diabolical sex acts committed against babies, toddlers and young people, yet we do not hear of special task forces set up to deal with "White on White" crime, I am not sure it is entirely helpful to 'racialise' crime.

We cannot deny the fact that in London, the majority of knife and gun crime is committed by young Black males (at least these are the cases that we read about in the papers). However, White people have their own fair share of it too. On June 2nd 2010, Derrick Bird, a self-employed taxi driver, went on a rampage in Cumbria killing 12 and injuring 11. All 12 victims were shot dead. Bird was not a gangster or a drug dealer.

On March 13th 1996, Thomas Hamilton entered a primary school in Dunblane, Scotland and opened fire and murdered in cold blood sixteen children and one adult. Again, like Bird he was not a drug dealer or gangster.

Gun crime is not new to the UK, the only difference is the way that it is reported. The reporting and responses to such crimes tend to bring out hidden racial prejudices when the crime is perpetrated by a person of colour. When the gunman is White, no inferences are made to their ethnicity or how they are corrupting the way of life in the UK.

Where Black gun crime is concerned, most times, the victims are known to each other and there is usually a history of animosity between the shooter and his victim(s). I have yet to come across a situation or incident where a Black gunman has opened fire and killed such a large number of people, Black or White for no apparent reason(at least not in the UK).

Recently, in Norway, Anders Breivik shot and murdered 69 people, I suspect if he had been a person of colour or a Muslim, the reporting and reprisals might have been somewhat different. The exploits of Raoul Moat are still fresh in the minds of the public, thankfully, Moat was not able to kill many people. Moat shot three people in two days and went on the run. His actions resulted in one of the largest manhunts in UK history, resulting in 160 armed officers being drafted in to apprehend him. Gun crime is not new to the UK or exclusive to a particular social or ethnic group, but certain elements of the population would have us think different. We can go back to the 50s and 60s when there were very few Black faces in London or the UK. The same sort of violence that we hear of today was being perpetrated by the Kray twins.

Violent crimes and murders have been committed since time immemorial and yet more often than not, when it involves a person of colour, ethnicity or race is usually made mention of as if that particular group or race has a proclivity or predisposition to crime.

Jack the Ripper caused mayhem from 1888-1891 in London's East End killing between 5-11 women (depending on which reports you read).

Peter Sutcliffe, also known as the Yorkshire Ripper went on a similar killing spree between 1969-1981, he murdered eleven women and attacked a further seven. Sutcliffe like anyone one else who commits such crimes was a monster, but his ethnicity was not seen as a factor to be made mention of in regards to these murders.

Harold Shipman, a medical doctor has 218 murders ascribed to him, if Shipman were Black, there would have been such a frenzy/ backlash, any Black doctor would automatically come under suspicion and patients would even refuse to be seen by them, we in the Black community do not have that luxury. I doubt that non-White people decided that they did not want to be seen by a White doctor in case they too were murdered or poisoned. It would have been understood that one person, one individual was responsible for such evil. Race and immigration would not have been used as factors and causes responsible for such crimes.

There are so many other high profile cases of violence, murders, rapes, robberies etc., but when viewed objectively, it can be seen that no particular ethnic group has a monopoly on crime, every single ethnic group is capable and responsible for some of the most horrendous crimes that have taken place on British soil.

How have we got to a situation where teenagers are running around the streets of London killing one another without fear of any sort of repercussion?

I have heard a lot of arguments put forward for the reasons that we have got to the position that we are in today, some say that poverty is the cause, other say that the kids have nothing to do. To some extent I suppose these reasons have a semblance of validity, but how about White kids who live in the same inner cities as these Black youths. Do they not also face poverty? Have their youth clubs not also being closed down? Why aren't they gunning themselves down?

I cannot claim to know the reason(s) why Black people have got themselves into such a mess but I believe there are steps we can take to make a difference.

People at times claim that poverty drives people to crime; there may be an element of truth to that, but I am not entirely sure. I once worked for a Housing Association and it transpired that one of our residents was a bank robber who had carried out numerous robberies, unfortunately, he and some of his colleagues went to rob a bank and things went disastrously wrong and he ended up getting shot and killed by the police.

The shooting brought about a lively discussion in the office, my take on things was that if he was really poor, not that I condone robbery or breaking the law, why not rob one bank and live off the proceeds. As the robbers were all young men, they were living the high life, fast cars, loose women, drugs and the like. It wasn't about trying to survive anymore, it was about pure criminality with regards to trying to live the high life.

Living in Nigeria, not only was I exposed to poverty, I experienced it myself. I can remember times going to bed hungry as there was no food to eat. One particular occasion is very vivid in my mind. My brother and I were both at university and we had run out of money and food. We had no money to go to Lagos to get money from our Dad, and our uncle whose house we were living in had not come home for the weekend. We were forced to go to my uncle's farm and get unripe plantain and make plantain chips. I remember we missed a few lectures, as we did not have any money to buy tickets for the university bus to shuttle us from where we were living to campus.

I left university in 1989 and coming from a polygamous home like many Nigerians, I was not too keen to go back to Lagos to a home set up that was not conducive. After my National Service which saw me teach English and History in a school in a very remote part of what was then Oyo state. I went to stay with my mum in a place called Ekundayo in Ogun state, which was a farming settlement. My mum had been forced to go there as she was kicked out of the house three years after we had come to Nigeria and my Dad had taken a second wife. He had taken all her belongings and possessions and refused to return them to her.

Ekundayo, was fun, but extremely hard work, I was living in a community where there was no electricity, running water or sanitary facilities, I was now a farmer growing and making cassava and other crops and staple foods.

Going to the toilet was fun, you would dig a hole in the ground with your cutlass, do what you needed to do and clean yourself with a banana leaf. Drinking water was sourced from the river and contact with the outside world was minimal as we had no access to newspapers or radio. It was against this backdrop that I returned to the UK in 1991.

Coming back to England was easier on some fronts; good roads, constant electricity, but my challenges were not over. Even though I had a degree to my name, I still could not get a job, for ten months, I was unemployed and could not even get a job in McDonald's. What kept me on the straight and narrow was my upbringing and the words of my mother, I remember her always saying to me, "remember the type of family you come from". Back then Black people had shame, even little things like eating in the street were frowned upon.

In 1995, my wife and I had been married almost two years and decided to sell everything we had and go to Africa to do missionary work, our travels took us to Nigeria, the Republic of Benin and South Africa.

In 1997, we came back to the UK with one suitcase to our name and about £100. My wife was also about five months pregnant and life was extremely difficult as we had to rebuild our lives from scratch. The church that sent us out on the missionary work were also not particularly helpful in helping us get back on our feet.

Despite all the difficulties we went through, we didn't break the law, turn to drugs or alcohol. I believed that if we worked hard and did the right thing, things would eventually improve.

I shared that part of our lives as at times people are too quick to use a hard life to defend crime.

I believe that education is a priority, we have to really make much more of an effort right from the very beginning, i.e. from primary school, yes there are some useless teachers out there, but a useless teacher is better than no teacher at all, I can remember times in Nigeria when we had no teacher for certain subjects, some children would mess around, but generally, we knuckled down and got into study groups and got on with things.

Even at times when we had a teacher, some teachers would send some of the students to the market to go and buy food for them or even give them the keys to their homes to go and clean their houses and in some cases make a meal for them.

In my final year of secondary school, I like many of my peers made sure that I had the syllabus for all the subjects I was about to take for my O Levels and studied hard so that I would be fully prepared. Life in Nigeria is/was hard. The majority of students knew that education was the only way out of poverty. Even back in the 80s. We would hear stories about Nigerians in the US with advanced degrees driving taxis. The fear and the drive to do well was therefore reinforced so that we had to take education seriously and do well in regards to the first major exams in our lives.

We have to get away from this crazy mindset that people who speak well or properly are trying to be White. We can't have it both ways, be ignorant and claim racism when employment cannot be found and then put down others who have taken the time and made sacrifices to better themselves, part of that being able to read, write and speak properly.

Having said that, I think it is a crime that in 21st century Britain, people can leave school and be semi-illiterate if not totally illiterate.

Emphasis from primary school should be placed on speaking and writing standard English, unfortunately what passes for English nowadays is the rubbish that is spoken on some of the soaps or reality TV.

Too many people are leaving both primary and secondary school unable to speak or write properly. Teachers are letting our children down by allowing them to incorporate slang and ghetto talk into their speech. By the time our kids get to secondary school the damage is already done. If the foundation is not in place, how can you build any further?

The irony of the whole situation is that kids today have so much information available to them. We had no internet in my time, I can remember saving up my dinner money when I was in Nigeria to buy books, we were not rich, but I knew the value of education. How many kids today, both Black and White, would deny themselves food to buy a book? The opposite is now the norm, a lot of kids are fat and obese and would not even dream of foregoing a hamburger or doughnut to buy a book.

Rather than having the conveyor belt education system we have in the UK whereby, even if you cannot write your name, you still get pushed into the next year, I think we should introduce what we had in Nigeria, students who have not attained a certain level of proficiency repeat the year until they have learnt the things they need to know.

The world is fast changing and it calls for literacy in all areas. You might be a genius on a PC but you still need to sell yourself by putting together a CV that makes sense and is not littered with grammatical and spelling errors.

Many years ago a friend and I would cringe every time we read about Black teens/youths being involved in crime; to some extent I think we took some comfort in the fact that the majority of the felons had 'English' names.

It was almost as if we as children or people of African descent were not involved in all that went on as we prided ourselves on the fact that African parents knew how to discipline their kids (boy do they know how) and our people would never get involved in such things. Fast forward 10-15 years, how wrong we were/are. So many of the kids now caught up in all this madness have African names, dare I say it, Nigerian names.

We claim to live in a civilised country, but I ask myself, how can it be that kids are killing kids in a supposed time of peace, Africa has many problems, but aside of war I have never heard of kids killing each other in times of peace.

I go back to one of my earlier points in that I believe that if it is possible, at some time Black youths should spend some time in their country of "origin". I know it did me a world of good, if I had stayed here from the ages of 14-24, there is no way I would have gone to university or be the person that I am today, I most likely would be one of the people that I am writing about.

Children need discipline and structure, something that this country has dispensed with. A lot of Black people have bought into this madness from their "cousins" across the Atlantic in saying "I don't need any man/woman". We are bringing kids by the truckload into single parent families (I have no problem with single parents where a spouse has died or a relationship has broken down). I do have a problem with kids producing kids who have no qualifications or means to support a child.

We are too busy tearing each other apart, running one another down for our kids to know what a healthy relationship is. Children have now become a means to a council house or getting extra money from the government or "Baby Father"(a term I despise with passion). Successive governments have helped to perpetuate fatherless households by withdrawing benefits from households where a father or father figure has been found to be in occupation.

I can remember trying to get a council property and so many people that I knew both Black and White would say, just move out of the property for a few weeks and get your wife to go to the Council and she will be given a flat or a house as you've got kids. I was seen as being stupid or not really being in need of housing as I refused to do it. It goes back to pride and upbringing, neither my wife nor I were raised that way, we were taught to do the right thing and always go through the proper channels. Trust me, it can be painful, when you are trying to do the right thing and you see people being rewarded for lying and cheating.

I go back to the issue of discipline, it starts with little things, such as school uniforms, most schools have a dress code that involves students having to wear a uniform, most of which consist of black shoes, what message as a parent are you giving when you allow your child to go to school in trainers. Invariably what you are saying is that what the school says is not important.

Some parents claim they have no money to buy proper school shoes for their children, but there always seems to be money for cable TV, flat screen TVs, gold teeth, bling and Nike trainers.

Teachers are unable to challenge these kids as mum or in some cases dad will come to school and give the teacher a verbal bashing if not a physical one.

From an early age, kids are growing up learning that there are rules, but these rules do not apply to them. Those that follow rules are dumb or stupid.

The same applies to hair, nowadays, boys are going to school with Afro combs in their hair, and all kinds of weird and wonderful haircuts and styles. If you want to do a fashion show, do it in your own time. The main reason for going to school is to get an education so that you can become a productive member of society. Unfortunately, we live in an age where the kids are right and the parents or elders are wrong, we are encouraged to not interfere and let the kids get on with it as they know best. The consequences of this softly, softly approach are all too obvious to see, unfortunately, we still persist with the madness.

I remember a few years ago, I was buying a pair of school shoes for my son who was probably around eight or nine at the time. We were a little stumped as to what to get him. Suddenly a woman came over who had probably seen we were in a bit of a dilemma and she pointed to a pair of shoes and said we should buy them as he would look so cool in school. I think she was rather taken aback by my response as I said he isn't going to school to look cool, he is going to school to get an education.

Too many Black teens and adults believe their self-worth comes from being cool or looking good and therefore struggle when they get into an environment where 'cool' is not needed.

How you dress and carry yourself is also of great importance, knowingly or unknowingly, you are projecting an image to people, your community, of who you are or how you want to be perceived. On many occasions I have seen young children, some as young as four or five dressed up to almost look like mini gangsters. The parents may seem to think it's cute for their "little man" to be all "grown up" with his gold chains, baseball cap back to front and his ridiculous haircut, but these actions usually have repercussions in later life.

T.V. has not really helped as everything is now so dumbed down that people who really shouldn't have access to the mass media are now on TV and are now put forward as role models for young impressionable Black people.

The thing that really hurts is that at present we are going through a time of deep economic crisis and so many Black people are coming into the job market unable to put a basic sentence together. Street slang and ghetto talk has become so embedded in the vocabulary of some of our kids that you can only cringe when they are conversing with people. They believe that they are coming across as cool and intelligent. Why have we as a people become so slack and lackadaisical and sat back and accepted all the rubbish that parades itself as Black culture which on the whole is destroying the fabric of our communities. Oftentimes this so-called Black culture amongst other negative things also seems to go hand in hand with criminal activity

Another thing that makes me laugh is that a lot of the so-called role models that our people look up to, who keep talking about "keeping it real"and being from the hood are making a killing out of the so-called community they are representing. For all their talk of being Gangsta and legit, where are the so-called role models living, they are not in the hood but living it up in the suburbs where the drive bys, muggings and rape are less frequent, if not, non-existent.

What are they giving back to their communities? They are making money from the impressionable kids who live in the "hood" but are doing nothing for the community. Now that the genie is out of the bottle and the Black man is on the verge of extinction (if current trends continue) what are they doing about the problem they have created?

We are now so desensitised to knifings and shootings that we don't really bat an eyelid anymore, people just now say, "did you hear about that kid that got killed the other day", as though we are talking about something as normal as going to the shop or having dinner. A child killing another child no longer outrages us anymore.

We claim we want the killings to stop and yet when a murder happens we insist on keeping quiet and harbouring the killers in the community – we can't have it both ways, violence only breeds more violence.

The downturn in the economy is only going to bring about more heartache. Muggings gone wrong, burglaries gone wrong, are going to leave more families minus loved ones.

I, like many people of my age, can remember getting a very

stern talking to or even at times a beating if I came home from school with something that wasn't mine. My mum or dad would ask me where I got the object in question from and if I could not provide a satisfactory answer, I was most likely going to end up with a sore behind. Today many parents know their son or daughter is not working, hasn't learnt a trade, but is driving a top of the range Range Rover or BMW or top model Golf but turn a blind eye and do not ask the questions that need to be asked as in some cases they themselves are benefitting from the dubious lifestyles their children are engaged in.

It is better to ask the questions and enforce a little discipline (not child abuse) while our children are young rather than wait for that phone call or home visit after your child hasn't been home for a few days, only to be told that a person fitting your child's description is in the morgue and you are needed to come and identify the corpse. Alternatively, you can watch while your child is being led to the cells to start a 15-25 year jail sentence. We always have choices and we have to decide whether or not we want to enforce them, the best choice is not always easy, but in the long run it does pay.

Just this week Barack Obama, the President of the United States of America visited Britain as part of his European tour, it was really funny seeing everyone fawning all over him, here is a Black man, the most powerful man on the planet and everyone, both Black and White cannot get enough of him, the man is smart, articulate, intelligent. He didn't get to the position of President as part of some affirmative action plan, but rather by working hard, applying himself and proving that Black people are just as smart as White people. No one group has a monopoly on knowledge.

Hopefully a lot of Black youths will be able to learn from him and decide to make something of their lives. Education is the key to progressing in life, we need to go back to the examples of our parents and grandparents who worked hard, studied hard and despite the odds and barriers against them still managed to make something of themselves. Why now that things are easier can't our people seem to make any progress? People are happy to walk to the shops in their pyjamas, curse in the street, wake up at midday, make no real effort to educate themselves and then get annoyed when society distances itself from them.

Just this week I met up with a friend who has temporarily relocated to Nigeria, I asked her how her son was doing in school, her son who is about nine now was doing terribly in school. I can remember how frustrated she used to be having to keep going to her son's school as his teachers would always be calling her to say he was up to one thing or another. Fast forward fifteen months he is now doing really well, he came fourth in his class and was so disappointed. Why is he doing so well? To put it in very basic, simplistic terms, we as Nigerians have always valued education, there are less distractions in Nigeria i.e. Xbox and the like, there are consequences for disobeying your parents, teachers, elders, life is also tough, there is no welfare or state handouts to be received if you are unemployed.

She also made me laugh when she said that she can just about carry his bag as the books inside are so heavy. Today in the UK, kids are pretty much congratulated for just coming to school. Why have we come to accept such mediocrity? We complain that foreigners are coming here to take our jobs, but what are we doing to stop this? Anyone who has an education or speaks or writes properly is pretty much held in contempt. If I was an employer and I had to choose between a foreigner who had a good work ethic, who wrote and spoke standard English or a home grown employee who was lazy, had an attitude problem and only spoke slang, I know who I would choose.

We need to make education a priority once again and regain a sense of pride and achievement. I can remember as a child a neighbour wanted to give my mum some clothes to give to my brothers, sister and I. My mother politely declined but afterwards was livid, she felt that the neighbour felt that she could not provide for her own family. The neighbour obviously meant well, but back then Black people had the right kind of pride, we took pride in buying things for ourselves and providing for our families all through honest hard work. We felt ashamed if a family member fell foul of the law. Today everything is so different, many are happy to live off welfare, happy to be ignorant, uncouth and check in and out of prison. We are fast running out of excuses. Why should we be this way? We have access to the same books as everyone else, we can go to libraries, we can access the internet, so why are we in the predicament that we are in today?

Today, I came across a truly disgraceful and horrifying statistic in the *Evening Standard* (a London newspaper), "One in three children in the capital (London) doesn't own a book, one in four pupils aged 11 cannot read or write properly". Another quote read, "The conveyor belt from illiteracy to exclusion to unemployment and, all too often criminality, is well documented. A recent prison reform trust study found 48 per cent of inmates had a reading age of a seven year old or younger; 85 per cent of 8-15 year olds have an Xbox."

The article does not give a breakdown of the ethnicity of the people, thankfully it does not apply to Black people only, however, I am sure that Black people are over-represented. The article also mentioned that in some schools teachers no longer correct children when they say things such as *aint* or *innit*, slang and ghetto talk have become the norm, everything is so dumbed down that when standard English is spoken, people struggle.

Personally, I do not see things improving as we continue to bombard our kids with horrible negative TV programmes and soaps, cool and stupid are given too much coverage, broken families are on the increase, drug and alcohol abuse is rife, anti-social behaviour is out of control, teenage pregnancies continue to rise, we glamorise gangsta rap and deceive ourselves that our kids are not affected by these things. If we pushed education as vigorously as any of the above, we might just be in a better place.

Recently, a working group/committee who dubiously call themselves the Elders have said that the war on drugs cannot be won, therefore we should legalise drugs. What will be next on the agenda, will we say that we cannot stop murder or paedophilia, so we might as well legalise both?

If we are to legalise drugs, it will be the Black community that again suffers more than most. Will shootings and murders decrease? Maybe, however, will our community be weaned off drugs? I doubt it, we will most likely find ourselves in the situation that because drugs are legal, more people will be tempted to try drugs and just become dependant on drugs without being criminalised.

To keep our kids from just becoming another statistic, we need to ensure that discipline is core to their upbringing, by discipline I am not just talking about chastisement for wrong doing, but discipline in so many areas, dressing appropriately for work and interviews. Knowing when to use standard English, getting to work on time, working hard to buy nice things, etc., etc.

Society at large also has a role to play, there needs to be more of a level playing field. For all the talk of equality and fairness, for many people of colour, it is not a reality. Very few people want handouts, most just want to know that they have a fair chance. Once equality and fairness come into play, things start to look different and people can be inspired by the differences they see.

People like Lewis Hamilton, the Williams sisters and Tiger Woods have done amazing things for the sports they represent, the impact they have had has probably made the playing field a bit more level for people of colour that have been inspired by them. Also if the playing field is level, there is also less of a need for people to become engaged in criminal activity.

If people can have access to good quality education and society, is fair, equal and transparent and parents play their part instilling values and expectations in their children, we might see a drop in the high numbers of Black people in jail or dying prematurely.

CHAPTER SEVEN

The riots of August 2011 were a complete eye opener to the disparity and despair of life in London. What could have started as a race riot quickly grew and descended into complete and total anarchy across London and to other major towns and cities across the UK.

What brought about the sudden and ferocious actions of the teens and youngsters involved. Many factors come into play, from allowing ghettos and areas of deprivation to take root, grow and become entrenched to the current economic climate we find ourselves in, which have seen the poor and disadvantaged become even more marginalised.

Many of the protagonists have said that they took part in the riot as they felt/feel the police do not respect them and have used the death of a young man in North London as an opportunity/excuse to vent their anger against the police.

I will try to discuss what I think are my ideas for the cause(s) of the riot as I think and believe they are many and varied.

Apart from the fact that a young man tragically lost his life at the hands of the police which was the catalyst for the riot(s), other factors played a part.

Many have said the riots are due to cuts and funding to local services being withdrawn, welfare benefit reform, the increase in tuition fees etc. There could be an element of truth to this and it may be a legitimate reason, but on this occasion I don't believe that this is a valid reason. I believe that people just got caught up in the summer madness and took advantage of the ineffectiveness and impotency of the police. I will however, concede that there are not many things for kids to do, youth clubs have been closed down, school fields have been sold off, community centres have also been closed down and seen funding cut.

A shocking factor that will not probably be discussed but I believe that has played a part without people knowing is the greed of the richest that has caused many residents to live in accommodation that is cramped and over crowded. We are often told that England, if not Great Britain, is over crowded and immigrants are swamping the country, but this could not be further from the truth.

I am currently reading a book that took me a long time to get my hands on as it was conveniently unavailable almost everywhere I tried to buy it, called, *Who owns Britain* by Kevin Cahill. The facts and statistics are quite shocking and show the greed and avarice of the richest in the UK. According to the book the UK is 60 million acres in size; 59 million people live on the land. Out of the 59 million, 189,000 families own 40 million acres of land, almost two thirds of the country. Who are the owners of this land; they are mainly Earls, Dukes and Barons with a close connection to the Royal Family. We claim to live in a democracy, but where the issue of land is concerned, in England we are still living in feudal times, we have just deceived everyone into thinking that we are all equal and that there is equality of opportunity.

What we find today is that Land is of a premium and the less fortunate (you and I) have to live in tiny houses, flats, apartments etc. while the rich and greedy 'land owners 'live in their sprawling estates. The writer also goes on to say how in 1066 William the Bastard, as he was called in France, arrived in England; he subjugated the land and its people and claimed everything as his own.

If you cramp people in tiny dwellings and oftentimes in dwellings that are not really fit for habitation, limit their opportunities, fail to invest in their communities, as sure as night follows day, protests and riots will follow.

Is it a crime to be rich? No. Is it a crime to be greedy? In my book yes, people become desensitised to the sufferings of those less fortunate than themselves and lack empathy and compassion. Why does an individual or family need 600 acres of land especially when such land is not used for farming purposes, unless land is equally redistributed or used more sensibly in England, more riots will continue.

I have discussed this point earlier, however, I am forced to return to it in terms of the riots, discipline has long been lacking in so many families for so long. For years now, right thinking people have been saying that discipline amongst most teenagers and youths is virtually non existent. Those of us who are old school and had the cane or slipper are seen as child abusers as we believe that children should be smacked (not abused) if they have done something wrong that is deserving of a smack. However, those of a more liberal disposition have labelled us as monsters etc. If a study were to be done on those that took part in the riots I am sure the majority of them would be found to have had no form of discipline in their lives whatsoever.

A White father of a son who was caught having taken part in the rioting/looting asked a reporter, "What can I do, I am not allowed to smack my child, I am not allow to tie him down, what can I do?" You have to pity a lot of parents who find themselves in that position, they want to be able to discipline (not abuse) their children but they in turn will be criminalised if they do. When the kids then go off the rails, everyone shouts, where are the parents?

I can remember in the early nineties when children/teens

who had broken the law would be sent on holidays rather than made to pay for their crimes (at the time, many of these schemes were aimed at White youth). What kind of message did this send?

I believe another factor is the materialistic mindset and obsession that people now have. People who earn 25k want to live a 75k lifestyle (gone are the days when people cut their cloth according to their size). Some have argued that poverty has played a part in the riots, to some extent that may be true, however, many that took part in the riots were kitted out in clothing that I myself as a working man cannot afford to buy.

Our children need to be made aware of the fact that your self-worth does not come from the clothes you wear but from the standards and morals that you as an individual have. It always amazes me, or should I say shocks and hurts me, the number of people that I come across who look good on the outside with their designer gear and the rest of the so-called paraphernalia that has come to "equate success", open their mouths to speak and a sentence which is clear, grammatical and correct cannot be heard. Parents do have a hard task on their hands as they are competing with a constant barrage of images from TV and magazines that are ramming the destructive ghetto/gangster lifestyle in the faces of our children.

I stated that I don't believe race played a part in the riot per se and I still hold that belief at least where the police are concerned (on this occasion), however, that is not to say that with regards to race relations all is well in the UK.

I went out to my town centre today, it being a Sunday morning in one of the areas that had been badly affected by the riots (Croydon) and on my way home going through an underpass I came across a White couple, probably in their late forties or early fifties. The wife (or partner) turned round, saw me and whispered to her husband, suddenly they quickened their pace. At the end of the underpass, they took one exit and I took another, we then met again as they were now getting into their car, the male then quickly looked at me and I flashed him a very sarcastic smile. It was a bit disheartening as they had probably judged me to be a mugger or some sort of miscreant.

My first impression was somewhat different, I had just viewed a middle-aged couple walking through an underpass, why was my initial perception not that as they were White, they must be racists or paedophiles. In their day to day lives they may be thoroughly decent human beings and not "racists" but their actions of today told a different story which was quite sad and which I feel will again become the norm in a lot of areas. I believe we will go backwards with regards to race relations and being Black will again become synonymous with being a criminal or being a potential criminal.

The criminal justice system (a bit of an ironic term to use as justice is rarely ever served) has played a part that has led to the riots we have seen. For years we have seen many young people being let off for crimes that really deserve a custodial sentence. Many of the people that come before the courts are repeat if not serial offenders, but rather than punish these people seriously, the courts just slap them on the wrist or if they do eventually go to prison, they are released half way through their sentence on an early release scheme. None of the governments want to build prisons as I guess it's not an election winner, but what is the alternative? Society is left to bear the brunt of having people in its midst who should be in jail rather than on the streets. Prison itself is a walk in the park, it's not a deterrent, and it's a bit of a luxury for those that eventually get there.

Education, or the lack of it, played a massive part in the riots, we have a generation of children, adults and parents that cannot read or write properly, for years it has been said that children are leaving school and at times colleges without basic literacy skills, teachers, parents and educators as well as the media have allowed for illiteracy, slang and just plain stupidity to co-exist with standard and grammatically correct English. A generation/ class has evolved that have no concept of how to read, write or speak properly and are therefore already doomed to a life of living on minimum wage as no employer in his or her right mind will employ someone who cannot read or write properly. When Tony Blair's government came into power, they came in on the back of the slogan "education, education, education". So much for education when kids cannot differentiate *whose* from *who's,* or *quay* from *key,* or *there* from *their*, *to* from *too* etc. The concept was good but it was doomed from the word go. As long as teachers have no power in the classroom, we can come up with slogan after slogan or build academy after academy; the result will always be the same, children leaving school without the basics in reading and writing.

In many respects the rioters have played right into the hands of the authorities. Tottenham, another one of the areas badly affected by the riots is an area I used to go to in regards to my line of work. I remember the first time I went there, about five or six years ago and I remember saying to colleagues that the place was so run-down. Now that the area has practically been burnt to the ground, the authorities will let the area remain like that for about five years and then start to redevelop the area. What will happen is that the area will now become gentrified and all the poor people, most of whom are minorities will be pushed further out of London. This in turn will now upset the racial demographics and dynamics of areas that they will be forced to move to.

Double standards and hypocrisy are always two things that irritate people and can at times bring out the worst in people. Some estimates have put the cost of the riots at around five hundred million pounds, however how many billions did the government use to bailout the banks? The financial crisis we now find ourselves in was caused by people who in the main have had the best education, live in the best areas and generally want for nothing. What was their punishment for the mess they put us in? Nothing. To make matters worse some of these people were even rewarded again financially for their incompetence and greed, as far as I am aware none were sent to prison.

Contrast their lot with those that took part in the riots. Many were Black, poor, illiterate or semi illiterate, live in the poorest areas and have probably never been on holiday. I do not justify the riots, however, when crimes are committed and double standards are employed, people will be aggrieved and find an avenue to vent their anger and frustration. The double standards employed here being that white collar crime usually perpetrated by Whites is usually dealt with less severely than street crime, which is usually perpetrated by Blacks. In financial terms white collar crime usually has a greater impact than street crime, but as it is less "personal" it seems to not be dealt with as severely as it should be. Everybody today is feeling the impact of the financial situation we now find ourselves in, not everyone has or will be a victim of street crime.

How many millions and billions have been spent on blowing up Iraq and Libya? Imagine if that money had been invested in poverty stricken communities, would it have solved all the ills we now face? No, but I believe it would have made a difference. Money can be found to prosecute wars overseas, but we cannot seem to find money to help the poor and dispossessed in our own backyard. As long as these double standards persist there will always be discontent that expresses itself as rebellion or riots or anti-social behaviour.

Not only is the spoken word important, image is just as

important, something, we as Black people don't seem to have figured out as yet. Students in England have only just started receiving their A Level results, this year is of great importance as from next year some universities will be charging £9,000 a year just for tuition fees.

Two young people were interviewed on the BBC, a White female and a Black male, I cannot remember the grades the girl achieved, however they were not as good as the young man who achieved three As, the young man did not really do himself any favours by appearing on national TV with his relaxed tinted hair and t-shirt, whereas the young lady was suitably attired for making an appearance on national TV.

Image and appearance are important, something the young man does not seem to have grasped, as of yet. If you are going to appear on national TV you have to make an effort to look good, too many Black people are too eager to appear on TV looking and sounding like they have never seen a mirror or been to school. This helps to perpetuate myths that people have about Black people that we are all dumb, illiterate, lazy and cannot speak well.

If you are a movie star, allowances can be made if you turn up on set or national television looking rather dishevelled as people will say that you are showing your creative side, or that you are a bit zany or eccentric. This latitude is generally extended to those who are White and not Black. A young man or woman who is Black and just starting out in life has to look good, well presented and groomed, especially if you want sixty million people to see you.

I remember a few years ago there was a debate in the *Metro*, a free London newspaper, about White people being given coverage during the Notting Hill carnival. A lot of Black people were unhappy as they felt that this was something that they as

Black people "owned". The carnival started almost fifty years ago in response to the racism West Indians faced when they arrived in England. It has now become a multi million pound two day event held over the Bank Holiday in August. Arguments were put forward for both cases, some felt that if Whites were not being given coverage, reverse racism was being played out, others felt that Blacks should be the only people shown as it was a Black event and represented the struggles that Black people faced and encountered when coming to these shores and they did not want that to be forgotten.

There has not been a debate about my next point, this is just a personal observation. When summer arrives in the UK, or at least the first hint of summer, some papers will generally show young ladies in their bikinis on a beach either strolling on the sand or just lapping up the rays of the sun with a caption like "four beauties basking in the twenty degree heat on Brighton beach" or something to that effect. Just as White people are in the minority at the Notting Hill carnival, Black women will also be in the minority when it comes to strolling along the beach in a bikini, however, there are some, but they never make the pages of the papers when summer comes. Even if you can't find Black women on the beach in a bikini, you will find Black families but we never seem to feature, why do we not see captions of, "A beautiful family enjoying the arrival of summer on Brighton beach,"(that beautiful family just happens to be Black). Inadvertently, or at least I hope so, the media perpetuates the biased concept of beauty; female, long hair and Caucasian.

We as Black people are concerned about how we look and are portrayed despite what the media may say or try and portray. Oftentimes when a Black person appears on TV a lot of my friends and I will dissect their appearance and unfortunately we have to cringe because more often than not they have "represented" us in the most stereotypical of ways that conforms to the views that White people have of Black people. (I guess we as Black people can also be our own harshest critics at times.) However, we don't just want to see urban Black people on T.V., sometimes we want to see well educated, well spoken Black people, not because they exist, but because we also want to see a more representative portrayal of the Black community.

Anybody who doubts the power of the media should look at Oprah Winfrey; she has used the media and its power to become an extremely powerful and successful woman.

Apart from being good at what she does, she also comes across as knowledgeable, articulate and employs what some may consider middle class values (decency, hard work, respect for authority etc. are not particular to any class or race).

We need to get back a sense of worth and shame, a few days after the riots, the cameras came out and reporters went about interviewing people and in one of the areas that had been affected a young Black man was interviewed and asked for his take on things. I was so disappointed with his response as yes, he did touch on the cuts that the government were making to benefits/welfare but what he was trying to infer was that the government was responsible for raising peoples' children. He said something to the effect that if a man has a girlfriend and she has a baby and then benefits are cut how is the baby to be supported. If you as a man or a woman want to bring a child into the world, you have to have the means to support the child and if at the time you don't, then you need to make plans to find ways to do so.

The state is there to help us when we fall on hard times, not to be a surrogate parent or a lifestyle choice, my parents' generation had pride and never really had the chance to rely on benefits as they were busy studying and working. Greater concern would have actually been securing accommodation as back then the "No Blacks, No Dogs, No Irish" signs were rife.

Many of the generation gone before must be disgusted how today's generation has become lazy and illiterate and so reliant on state benefits to live.

If anything, the riots have shown what happens when things are on the decline and people speak up but the powers that be fail to listen, people have spoken about the inequality in society, family breakdown, moral breakdown etc. for years but all the government says when something happens such as a shooting or a mugging or a rape is that this is just an "isolated incident". Well how isolated were the riots?

The government now wants to be seen as taking a hard line in tackling the yobs who partook in the riot but that ship has already sailed. We are told that some may lose their benefits; others may lose the council homes that they live in. What happens when someone who already is on the fringes of society has lost their home or has their benefit taken from them? Twenty, thirty years ago when people were talking about unruly kids, what did the police, government and judiciary do? If a strong message was sent out then, maybe an impact might have been made. The cynic in me says that as the majority, if not all, of these incidents (gun and knife crime) took place in areas that were not representative of England's green and pleasant land, the powers that be were not really too concerned. Now that we see branches of Miss Selfridge's and the like going up in flames people are beginning to sit up and take notice.

A week after the riots, things have returned to "normal"; a fourteen-year-old boy was stabbed to death in a park in North London. Another fourteen-year-old has been arrested on suspicion of the murder, but what will happen to him? As far as I am concerned, if you take a life, you in turn should spend the rest of your natural life behind bars. We need to take radical action as we will fast find ourselves like America where the majority of young Black males in the inner cities are either dead or in jail.

We need to see more representation of Black people in all walks of life, my line of work requires that I attend court quite regularly, in my more than ten years of going to court I have only come across two Black judges which I think is pitiful. If the police were labelled as institutionally racist, what are we to say about the legal profession itself? I personally know so many people who have studied Law, Accountancy, Engineering, etc. They are not stupid and yet they are not at the top of their profession, if there are deficiencies where are the mentoring programmes to help people of colour to become partners in law firms or consultants and judges.

People don't want hand outs, just a level playing field, hence the apathy of some Black youth to education, they have seen their parents work and study hard only to see them working on the buses with a Masters degree or driving a cab. Even though this has been the case and is still sometimes the case we must continue to strive for a quality education, as is said, the pen is mightier than the sword, education can and always will open so many doors, even if the doors are sometimes intentionally locked.

Another reason that has been given for the riots is the relationship that a lot of young people have with the police, especially Black people. To be honest I was not going to list this as a cause, as in my limited experience I have had very little interaction with the police, i.e. I have never been arrested and I do not have a criminal record. My desire is that this is a claim that I can and always will be able to make. As a child that grew up in Britain in the 70s and early 80s, my desire to connect with the police has not diminished.

Over the years, I suppose I have been trying to deal with my issues with the police, I have also tried to do what is right; however, my relationship with the police has suffered a further set back.

Recently, we had a barbecue to thank everyone who helped us moved house as we finally have now moved. We have moved into a very nice property which is located within a close and there are less than ten houses in the close. In total, we probably had about twelve adults and four children in attendance.

The children ranged in age from about 5–14 years in age, one of the children came inside to say that there was a police car outside, I went outside and enquired of the officer what the matter was, he informed me that they had a report of a fight, the children were all getting on fine and were actually playing on their scooters and just talking to one another.

I informed the officer that there may have been a fight somewhere else, close to where we live, however in the close where our property is situated all was well, I think he mentioned that they had already been to an incident where I said the altercation may have taken place, then suddenly he said why are all these kids out on the street at 9.50pm (this was a Saturday evening, since moving here, my son is normally indoors by 9pm, but as his cousins were around and all the kids were out having a good time, we thought they could stay out a little longer, it was also the summer holidays as well).

I informed him that they were not out in the street but in the close, when his demeanour changed and he became very aggressive and rude. I think we went back and forth about three times when my wife intervened and told me to forget it, which I did and left the situation. However, I was really upset about the whole encounter as I thought there was no need for the officer to be rude and aggressive, I had actually come out with the intention of trying to help and assist only to be met by an obviously poorly educated police officer who probably felt that a well spoken Black man had shown him up for his ignorance, he probably felt that I was being a bit uppity and had forgotten my place.

I guess that he had never come across a Black man with a bit of grey matter, my niece who was also present, who is mixed race and lives in a very predominately monochromatic environment and is twelve said that the police are always aggressive with Black people. I did my best to assure her that this was not the case as I did not/do not want her to have the same issues as I have.

I often wondered in the past why people were reluctant or reticent to help the police and now I know why. Unfortunately first impressions count and not all the police are bad, however, the officer that I spoke with was a terrible representative of the police and has destroyed the little progress I had made in trying to conquer my feelings about the police.

Two weeks after the riots, you would think that the police would try their best to try and build bridges with the local communities and not try and make things worse.

I think my issues with the police stem from my own experience growing up, like my niece, my siblings and I also grew up in a monochromatic environment and I can remember an incident that happened in the early seventies. The four of us were on our way home from school and we used to take a shortcut home through a place called the "Dell". It was summer time and kids being kids had set fire to a patch of dry grass prior to our passing through, by the time we passed, the fire had burnt out or had been put out by the fire brigade, as we passed through, we were stopped by a police officer who said that they had been informed that four Black boys had started the fire, apparently we had been "identified" by a woman who had seen us from her back garden.

Even though my sister was in a skirt, the police man still took it upon himself to give us a hard time, back then kids still had a fear of authority, especially the police. I was still in primary school at the time and more than thirty-five years later that incident is still vivid in my mind. He was acting upon clearly invalid intelligence but still decided to abuse the power that he had as he was probably affronted that Black people could live in an area that was 99.9% White.

Another incident that has stayed with me occurred when I was about twelve years old, a friend and I went for a bike ride still within the vicinity of the area in which we lived and we rode past a boat club where a lot of boats were moored. We often used to play in the area, as we also had a friend who lived about a one minute walk from the boat club, apart from riding our bikes there, we would also skim stones across the river.

A policeman approached my friend and I who was White, as were all my friends were, as there were no Black people in Thames Ditton in the 70s/early 80s and he stopped us and asked us what we knew about a boat that allegedly had been set on fire. As we knew nothing about the incident we pleaded innocence, his response to that was, "Did it happen by Black magic?" About thirty-three years later, I still remember that quote as if it were yesterday, to make matters worse, when he uttered the quote, he turned and looked at me.

I will confess that as a kid, I had a bit of a reputation and oftentimes, things were attributed to my friends and I and we too would milk and embellish the notoriety that was attributed to us, but on this occasion we were innocent.

Inertia and inactivity has also led us to the place we find ourselves in today. David Cameron, the British Prime Minister is talking tough and says that the government will deal with the 120,000 problem families. He is also talking about the need to re–introduce discipline back into the classroom. Firstly, where does the statistic of 120,000 problem families come from and if it is the case that there are 120,00 problem families, why has it taken a riot for the government to wake up and realise something needs to be done?

The problem families that have been identified are probably reliant on benefits – if their benefits are cut or removed, how do they survive? It will lead to a further downward spiral in their behaviour and we cannot jail them as the jails are full, so really, not much can be done about these problem families. The politicians will continue to talk tough and nothing will really come of it.

With regards to discipline, we have lost that battle, the genie is out of the bottle and discipline in schools will not be the same again, we have become a society where common sense no longer prevails, children are given unbridled rights and privileges and we then complain when things go wrong. What can the future hold for a child who has no education, knows no barriers and has never really had any discipline instilled or inculcated?

Finally, we talk about England or the UK having a Christian heritage, but where is God in what we profess? I sometime laugh when I hear the National Anthem being sung as I say who really believes in God today. I am not one to force religion on anyone or to say that there is only room for a monotheistic belief to be held, but a belief/way of life that was part of the fabric/culture/heritage of the UK is now almost dead. Shops are opened on Sundays all in a bid to make more money, people are therefore taken away from their families or loved ones for longer periods of time; we already work the longest hours in Europe.

Churches are empty and some have even been converted to flats; a friend and I recently passed by one such conversion and he was quite saddened (he happens to be Catholic) and we discussed amongst ourselves and said it would be unimaginable for a Mosque to be converted into a block of flats. Muslims would never allow for such a thing to happen, but we in the UK are happy to throw away our tradition and heritage and then blame ethnic minorities.

Assembly is no longer relevant in schools and God has been driven out of the classroom. Religion that is not fanatical or dogmatic has a place in society but we seem to have forgotten that. Americans are not afraid to show their belief in God, but we in the UK don't seem to have that same conviction, I suppose that it is always easier to blame someone else for the erosion of your culture/heritage than to look closer to home. Where there is a void or vacuum, sooner or later something comes along to fill it. As the Bible says, "you reap what you sow".

Funnily enough, I just watched a programme on the BBC this morning and part of the debate was whether Muslims in the UK are now being demonised, especially after the events of 9/11. The panel consisted of three people, one of whom is a journalist for a newspaper called the *Daily Mail* (some consider the paper to be quite right wing). His argument was that the UK is a Christian country and that it has an Anglo-Saxon heritage and that the predominant host culture must be preserved, none of which in my view is wrong, however this same individual I very much doubt would espouse the same view if we used his same logic to say the same about America. Should we therefore say that all Americans must know and speak Native American Indian dialects?

Part of the problem with the above is that these views are only convenient when put forward from a Eurocentric/ Western viewpoint, the very thing that he was against, i.e. British/English values being taken over is the very thing that the British and English and other Europeans did when they went to other lands – not only did they displace the cultures and traditions they met, they also killed a lot of people in the process. Another one of the panellists, a woman who claimed to be Jewish, countered the argument of the third panellist, a Muslim who made mention of the Crusades by saying that happened a long time ago. Arguments like hers are most unhelpful as they try to diminish the impact of things that have happened. Would she say to an assault victim that he or she was a victim of an assault thirty years ago, they should get over it as it was a long time ago?

I very much doubt that the journalist from the *Mail* would have spoken with the same conviction with regards to apartheid South Africa, a minority group, imposed their way of life and language upon a majority and when they tried to throw off their oppression they were called terrorists.

The real enemy of Christianity in the UK is not those wishing to impose Sharia law, it is the White Anglo-Saxon community itself. When British Airways suspends members of staff for wearing crucifixes as a symbol of their faith (not that the Bible teaches that one has to do so). Or when schools cannot celebrate Christmas or Easter, the people that come up with this madness are White.

It is not ethnic minorities trying to sound a death knell for Christianity in the UK. The current ongoing sex scandal in the Catholic Church has nothing to do with minorities, again, in the main, White Caucasian bishops, priests and reverend fathers have damaged the standing of the Church. The decline in Church attendance is not down to ethnic minorities; those wishing to turn the UK into a secular society/state are in fact those that would claim to be indigenous to these shores.

I read another story today in one of the newspapers in which a man with proven links and knowledge of the 7/7 bombings in London will not be repatriated to Somalia as it would be a breach of his human rights. The idiots who make these decisions again are predominately all male and all White. Someone who has a deep hatred of what the UK stands for is given leave to remain here indefinitely, common sense would dictate that if you are a foreign national and try and blow up people you should be deported, others have been deported for less.

My mother came to the UK in the early 60s and qualified and worked as a nurse for some time. She went back to Nigeria for good in 1982. I got married in 1993 and had to send a letter of invitation for my mother to come for my wedding here in the UK, my mother was refused a visa and missed my wedding. My mother, like many Africans and West Indians were invited to the UK in the 60s, they were part of the Commonwealth, she has/had no criminal record, she paid taxes for well over twenty years and yet was refused a visa to attend her son's wedding, whereas a known terrorist from Somalia can be given the right to remain in the UK because sending him back to his country would breach his human rights. Madness and stupidity prevail all over the UK today.

The British had a good run in Nigeria, in fact they were there for 99 years, from when a British protectorate was formed in 1860 (Lagos) to when Nigeria was finally granted independence in 1961. They got natural resources and manpower on the cheap if not for free. British West Africa contributed to the economic well-being of the UK as did the slave trade and yet individuals of these nations who helped the

UK to be what it is today are not allowed to visit their loved ones who happen to be resident here.

Double standards like these always leave a bitter taste in the mouths of both Black and White alike.

Ethnic minorities did not ask for God to be kicked out of morning assembly in schools, we do not have the political power to do so; the majority of ethnic minorities have a strong belief in God, hence the proliferation of Evangelical/Pentecostal Churches in this country.

The Church traditionally has been the bedrock of the Black community especially in the United States, to some extent, the Church was the same for newly arrived immigrants to this country, unfortunately, this cannot now be said to be true, yes there are lot of "Black" Churches springing up but many are now preaching a perverted version of the gospel, what I term a "prosperity Gospel". They preach about getting rich quick, but there is no obligation for the adherents to live a righteous life, God is now reduced to an unscrupulous businessman who rewards you financially for a life that is not subject to financial or moral regulation.

The Church now to a certain extent is a mockery of what is used to be, pastors and reverends wearing suits of several thousand pounds, continue to fleece their gullible congregations of their hard earned money to fund their ungodly and lucrative lifestyles. Like the paedophiles in the Catholic Church, they ruin the name of God in the Black Church.

We now have a generation of Black people growing up who have no faith in God. When a generation, people or community have no faith in God or a higher power, no boundaries, no respect, no concern for their fellow man, a 'me, myself and I' mindset is all that matters, the road ahead will be rocky.

The riots cannot be condoned; however, they showed that

if people are neglected and forgotten, anarchy is not usually far away. Some reports did try and focus on the number of Black and Brown faces that took part in the riot(s), however. Some of the factors that brought about the discontent are not too dissimilar to the same factors that brought about the peasants revolt of 1381, led by Wat Tyler.

Riots and rebellions have been taking place way before Black people arrived in the UK. The real reasons for the riots are those that have been listed and more and not immigration as some would have us believe.

CHAPTER EIGHT

In many respects, relationships are the building blocks of society, where healthy relationships are absent, trouble is not far behind.

Recently, I was on my way home, having stayed late to catch up on some work. I was on the second leg of my journey, which consisted of me taking a tram to reach my destination.

Two young Black boys still both in their school uniform (this was about 7.30pm) were talking and one said to the other, "she was asking to be f★★★★d". These boys were probably about fourteen-years-old if that.

I tried to cast my mind back to when I was fourteen, yes I was not that naïve to not know about sex, however, I was not so vulgar and uncouth to use such language in public or on public transport. My saving grace could have been that at fourteen, I had been uprooted from the UK and taken to Nigeria. As I have mentioned earlier, Nigeria was a total different ball game to the UK, for all its issues. Nigeria was a place where respect, decency and good upbringing were paramount.

If, as a fourteen-year-old, I were to use such language in public, I would be shouted down, if not given a slapping by a total stranger. As a fourteen-year-old in Nigeria, my main focus was adapting to a new culture and environment and making sure my grades were good enough to secure promotion to the next class. I also had to contend with constant power failures, malaria, avoiding a whipping in school – be it for being late, poor work or for my uniform not being ironed properly.

I sat and looked across at the two boys and thought they

are symptomatic of what is wrong about a lot of Black boys today (White kids without a shadow of a doubt will also be involved in this kind of conversation, however, as in most cases, our kids are always seem to be over-represented in negative things).

They were rude, they looked dishevelled in what passed for their school uniform and obviously really had no real concept of what sex or rape was about or meant.

I think I felt both sad and disgusted by them; sad that they probably thought they were "men" as they were having sex, and disgusted that their manners were appalling. I also wondered why they were not home at a decent hour. I can remember as a sixteen year old, my father saying that before I left the house I had to inform him and sitting just across from me were two kids with attitude and big mouths who probably answered to no one either at home or school.

When it comes to relationships, we in the Black community are not doing too well, too many of our kids are being born into and raised in single parent families and a lot of our kids have no understanding of what a healthy or normal relationship is or should be, hence my observing what I did with those two boys.

Sex has become so cheapened and means nothing, why shouldn't it when women, Black women, are portrayed as gold digging ho's and Black men are portrayed as hardcore, ghetto super studs. Why build or invest in a relationship when "all" men are dogs and "all" women are money grabbing ho's. Sex is used as a bargaining tool, no intimacy or affections are involved; it's about being used.

The hardcore, ghetto man cannot show his emotions as real men don't do that, the "strong Black woman" also doesn't show her emotions as if she does this is seen as a sign of weakness which means that she is a soft touch.

Both feel that they are in a position of power, as at the end of the day they can both walk at any time, kids or no kids. If you have two emotionally stunted people coming together to try and form a relationship, things at best will be tricky.

I have always said there is no such thing as the perfect relationship or marriage, you have good relationships and good marriages, anyone who says otherwise is either a very good liar or delusional.

Relationships that are built on anything other than love more often than not will fail. If we as Black people have now conditioned ourselves to not be able to love one another but to be antagonistic to each other, how are our relationships going to thrive? You can't build a relationship on violence, criminal behaviour or petty theft.

If we are unable to express emotions such as love, tenderness, intimacy and compassion, the relationships we build will not be lasting ones.

We recently moved house about three months ago, prior to our moving, every Friday we would pick up a meal at our local West Indian takeaway. Once while we were waiting for our order to be taken, a middle-aged man came into the shop and in his lovely Jamaican accent, started saying, he didn't know what was wrong with Black people. He said that if you see a Black man with a White woman, you will see them holding hands in the street and everywhere they go the Black man will make her feel extra special. He then asked why it isn't the same when a Black man and woman are together; he said you won't see the Black man walking the woman down the street like a princess.

His comment cannot be taken to represent the state of all Black relationships, however, I said to myself that he had a point, how many Black people do I see showing genuine affection to themselves when walking in the street, I don't really see many.

Could part of the issue be the music we listen to that promotes thuggish and violent behaviour, how can a man show affection to a woman, when she is nothing better than a money grabbing, gold digging ho. In less than twenty years, our beautiful African queens have suddenly become ho's.

We went out today and I was playing a CD in the car of some songs that I had put together, Alexander O'Neal and Cherelle – 'Saturday Love', 'Midnight Star' – 'Curious, Joy and Pain' – Maze. My wife looked over at me and said "this is what I call music".

Just as I parked the car, Roberta Flack came on singing 'Back together again', I switched off the engine and was getting out of the car and my wife just sat there, I said to her "aren't you getting out" she said that she was quite happy to just sit in the car and listen to the music, that's the power of great music.

When I listen to "Black music" of the eighties and early nineties, it just reminds me of good times and great memories. Talking of the power of great music, one of the first cassettes I bought my wife-to-be (we had no CDs back then) was the aptly titled, 'The Power of Great Music' by James Ingram, almost twenty years later she still has the cassette, I have since moved with the times and bought her the CD.

Where are the singers like James Ingram today? There isn't a market for great singers singing great songs that are positive and talk about positive healthy romantic relationships. All we have for our very impressionable Black youths are generally very violent, misogynistic and crude songs. We then wonder why many relationships that our people have are often violent, short lived and shallow.

The explosion of single parent families within the Black community is having a catastrophic impact, so many of our kids (not all single parent families are problematic either) now belong to single parent/single income families. Is it any wonder why a lot of them have discipline issues or resort to crime? I know when I was acting up as a teenager, my Dad was in Nigeria at the time and my Mum was busy doing two or three jobs trying to provide for four kids. Until very recently, single parent families were an alien concept to Africa, we have now bought into/are buying into the single parent trap and it is hurting us.

I don't see things getting any better either, we live now in an age where almost all kids have access to a Blackberry, iPod or smartphone and children have access to all kinds of music and pornography. On the way to school and back home, our children are listening to a lot of music, which is not particularly beneficial. It's a bit like junk food, if you gorge on junk food it will have an impact on your body.

What is a healthy relationship? Unfortunately, we do not seem to have an understanding what the term means or is. Too many of us settle for anything in a pair of trousers or a skirt so as not to be lonely. Behind closed doors all sorts of horrors take place and yet we stick with these so called partners, husbands and wives. How have we come to accept domestic abuse, thuggish behaviour and infidelity as the norm? (Again this does not describe all Black relationships, but there are too many like this.)

It all goes back to standards, if you don't have any respect or standards for yourself, how can you expect others to treat you with respect?

Relationships are tricky, but ground rules have to be established from the start. Almost from day one, my wife and I decided that no family member on either side would be allowed to intervene in our relationship. On occasion I have had to have a few stern conversations with my mother about things that have been said. Many men are found wanting in this area, they allow their mothers to say almost anything to their partners/wives.

My mother, has done her part, she raised me, provided for me, taught me right from wrong etc. However, I am no longer under her roof, I have the utmost respect for my mother, however, I cannot, do not and will not allow for her to upset my wife.

When I first met my wife, from the very first date that we went on, I knew I had met the woman I was going to marry. I remember rushing home and announcing to my flat mates that I had met the woman I was going to marry. However it would be another eighteen months from our initial date to marriage. Ground rules and expectations had to be established, those seventeen months were vital, there were lots of disagreements and differences and at one point we almost called it quits, however almost twenty years later, touch wood, we are still together. Apart from the love that we have, respect and ground rules have played a prominent part in keeping the relationship going.

It hasn't been an easy twenty years either, we have had our fair share of trials and tribulations.

One of the good things about African family set ups is the role that elders often play. I can remember being quite shocked when I first got to Nigeria seeing grown men and women being given a telling off for some misdemeanour or other and oftentimes having to apologise. Where family disputes or relationship matters are concerned, elders often play a pivotal role in helping to resolve matters. Most issues that young married couples go through, they have experienced and at times have the answers to help resolve the dispute.

It is by no means a perfect solution and not all the advice is correct or relevant, but it does help couples to look at things more objectively and with a clearer head, rather than taking the easy route and just giving up and walking away.

How long this will continue to be the norm, I cannot say as again, Western culture and values begin to permeate and pervade African cultures and societies. Currently in the UK many older citizens are having to sell their homes to pay for their care. In most African countries, there are no such things as old people's homes as the older folk are still considered as an integral part of the family and either live on their own or with other family members.

Watch any television talk show and you will see just how dysfunctional families, both Black and White, have become. Most of what passes for soaps in the UK are just programmes where people shout a lot, are of limited education and are having the odd affair here or there. It all boils down to lazy programming and lack of ideas. For years shows like CSI and Law & Order have kept us captivated, the shows are well written, well acted and production is of a very high standard.

Black people are not incapable of having long lasting healthy relationships, however, the so-called "Black culture" that many of us have adopted is not what will help us to build the stable households that our children need to be able to thrive and compete with others.

CHAPTER NINE

I have very fond memories of Nigeria, however, I also have memories that are not so fond and are quite disappointing.

Depending on where you get your information, Nigeria has a population of between 100-170 million people and between 250-501 languages and dialects.

Nigerians are as diverse as the geography of the country, a popular misconception that those who have a limited knowledge of Nigeria is that there is such a language as Nigerian: the three main languages spoken in Nigeria are Hausa, Yoruba and Igbo. These three languages have no similarities and therefore if you want to be able to converse with all Nigerians, one has to be proficient in Pidgin English. Just as the West Indians have their Patois, we have our Pidgin English, a language which to some degree unifies all Nigerians.

When I first arrived in Nigeria in 1981, Nigeria's main issues were no light (electricity), no water, no good roads. When I left Nigeria in 1991, Nigeria's main issues were, no light, no water, no good roads. In 2015, the scenario is the same, no light, no water, no good roads.

In thirty-four years the three most basic things that a society/country needs to develop and progress have remained stagnant if not deteriorated. I should have also included health care, but I will touch on that later on.

In the ten years that I was absent from the UK, many changes had occurred, so much so that it took me a few months to readjust to things when I came back. Nigeria reminds me of a comment that one of my school teachers wrote in my school report, "Bola has much potential but unfortunately dedicates too much of his time to disruption and silly behaviour". Talk to any Nigerian and the word potential will always be made mention of with regards to Nigeria's development or growth.

In many respects, the talk of potential is not a pipe dream, however, what has prevented Nigeria from becoming one of the best countries in the world.

As I have said earlier, you cannot condemn an entire race or people because of certain actions or traits, however when certain actions or traits are overwhelmingly prevalent an observation or "judgement" can be made.

Corruption has done untold damage to Nigeria, from the most basic of things such as driving your car on the road to trying to get hospital treatment or pass through immigration one is confronted by corruption and bribery at every turn.

Corruption has crippled every facet of Nigerian life, and destroyed the country, those wishing to live an honest life are left frustrated or if able are forced to leave the country, hence the massive brain drain. Nigerian doctors, lawyers, accountants, engineers etc. are boosting and making massive contributions to the economies of other nations because corruption does not allow for them to make a contribution to their own country.

Money earmarked for construction of roads, clinics hospitals, schools etc. never finds its way to where it needs to go, it usually ends up in the pockets of government ministers and other parasitic sycophants.

Since the discovery of oil, something in the region of four hundred billion dollars has been stolen and misappropriated, imagine if this money had actually gone to building schools or investing in communities, what a different country Nigeria would be. Many Nigerians will comment about how beautiful Dubai is, Dubai has oil and has invested its oil money wisely.

Nigeria has squandered its money on rubbish and lined the pockets of the most reprehensible and unpatriotic of Nigerians.

A popular saying amongst many Nigerians is that your average Nigerian is too selfish to sacrifice himself/herself for something noble. Imagine the shock and horror when we first heard about the underpants bomber, many at first believed that he could not be a Nigerian as which Nigerian would give up his life for something he believed in (killing innocent people is by no means a noble cause, rather I use the analogy to show the selfishness of the average Nigerian). In many respects the statement is true, many Arab countries have now thrown off the yoke of oppressive leaders and regimes, Nigerians will continue to complain and beseech God to do everything on their behalf, but we will not be prepared to put our necks on the line to stand up for something we believe in.

I remember talking with an uncle just before coming back to the UK and he asked why I wanted to go back, his words were "Nigeria is the easiest place to become a millionaire", which was and is probably true if you are prepared to compromise your morals and principles (not everyone who has made it in Nigeria has done it through dubious means, but a fair few have).

As a naïve twenty-two-year-old I remember thinking that corruption was non-existent in the UK. Time, age and experience have now proved to be great teachers. When I graduated from university, my dad said that he could get me a job in a merchant bank, I resisted passionately, saying that as a history graduate I would be denying someone who actually studied accountancy or banking his or her rightful place, I stuck to my guns and came back to the UK, as I said earlier, time, age and experience are great teachers.

Corruption abounds everywhere, however in the West it is

not on the scale that leads to the crippling of an entire nation. Imagine British Airways going out of business due to embezzlement and corruption, Nigeria once had its own national carrier, Nigerian Airways, but due to corruption, mismanagement and the like it folded and went out of business like so many Nigerian run/owned businesses.

I made mention of the health service; we have no idea how fortunate we are in the UK with regards to the National Health Service. In Nigeria, you have to pay for any kind of treatment, I have heard too many horror stories of people dying because they could not come up with the funds to be treated. Hospitals and clinics are awash with fake drugs, I can actually remember times going to chemists to buy medicine and being asked whether I wanted the original or the fake. It would be funny if it wasn't true, why on earth would I want to buy fake drugs if I was ill?

What I find particularly shameful and scandalous and extremely embarrassing is the fact that any time the Head of State is ill, he will be flown to either America, Germany or Saudi Arabia for treatment. Can you imagine the President of the United States being flown to Europe for medical attention due to medical facilities not being available in America to treat him? There would be an uproar. That's how it is in Nigeria, we have no decent hospitals and have to fly our heads of states to various countries for treatment. A few billion dollars could build a state of the art hospital, not only for the Head of State but also for the general populace, but we are so short sighted, selfish and greedy, that we would rather amass millions and billions in Swiss bank accounts than try and do anything for the country.

Nigeria hasn't always being a joke. In the early 70s Nigeria's finance minister went on record to say that Nigeria's problem was not how to make money but how to spend it, civil servants were given bonuses and increased payments and Nigeria in many respects became a world power, at least economically. Due to the increase in wealth of the average Nigerian, many Nigerians were able to circumvent the law that tried to deal with congestion on Lagos island by buying two cars with both odd and even number plates, thus enabling them to get to the island on any day of the week.

However, this golden era was short lived, by the 80s Nigeria had become a pauper nation, making several trips to the world bank for loan upon loan. Corruption had become endemic and a massive brain drain that continues to this day began.

Anyone who had any moral fibre and was not infected by corruption had to find some way of leaving the country. Cronyism and tribalism saw illiterates and semi-illiterates appointed to positions of power and influence and a once great country began to crumble and implode.

The government to some extent saw what was happening, but could not wean itself off its diet of greed and corruption and resorted to gimmicks to stem the mass exodus of Nigeria's brightest and best. I remember an advert depicting a man at the airport saying that he had had enough of the country and was checking out, the advert concluded with the words, "Andrew no check out O". The ad was meant to appeal to the patriotic nature of Nigerians urging them to not leave the country, but to rather stay and rebuild the country.

Who in their right mind would stay in a country that had no electricity, poor health facilities, no decent roads and was bedevilled by military coups?

Since then Nigeria has spiralled and descended into a very dark and ugly place and in my opinion has passed the point of no return. Today, corruption has reached stratospheric levels, greed and deception by "419" churches is on an unprecedented level, ritual killings and murders is the norm and now Islamic extremism, coupled with almost daily bombings and assassinations are common place. Nigeria's real God – money – gathers daily converts who will stop at nothing to become big men and madams who are willing to do anything to become rich.

People who can barely string a sentence together are feted and treated like royalty and are appointed to positions of great importance and responsibility, their only ability being able to steal millions and billions of dollars.

Unfortunately, the above was played out right in front of me thus giving me first hand experience. I last visited Nigeria in 1996 and since that time have not been back. As I have a British passport, the cost of a visa plus charges would cost me about £200. I therefore decided to apply for a Nigerian passport. The cost of a Nigerian passport according to the website of the Nigerian High Commission is $65 plus an additional £20 payable by postal order.

I had tried several times to apply online, unfortunately, as with most things with regards to Nigeria things are never straightforward, applying for a passport being one of them. After several searches on Google I managed to find a telephone number of the organisation that acted on behalf of the Nigerian High Commission, which happened to be based in New York and were in my book as equally as useless as the people they claimed to be acting on behalf of. Customer service was non-existent, no complaints procedure existed.

I was eventually told that if I had problems with online payments I should visit the Nigerian High Commission and I would be able to make payment once I got there.

On my arrival there I was met with the usual Nigerian set up, poorly trained and barely literate individuals intoxicated by a minuscule amount of power and authority. People were being shouted at and spoken to in the most offensive of ways. Nigeria is a very complex place with complex problems, everyone in Nigeria wants to be a "big man" or "madam" and is eager to let you know how important they are. Nobody in Nigeria is Mr or Mrs, most Nigerians will have a title in front of their name, i.e. Lawyer, Engineer, Alhaji, Alhaja, Professor, Accountant also followed by their educational qualifications. It is therefore of no surprise to see someone introduced as Chief, Engineer, Dr....Phd. M.Sc. MPhil. B.Sc. At the root of all of this need to look or seem important is a very deep rooted inferiority complex.

Having endured the usual abuse of power, I eventually managed to explain my plight and gain access to the High Commission and pay for my Passport, however, once inside I again had to endure another round of insults that ordinarily I would not tolerate. I relayed my experience to a friend and stated that it made me really sad as I don't want to be classist, elitist or superior, however, if I were in Nigeria, the goons that they had on the door treating people like animals would not be the kind of people that I would associate with.

I go back to my earlier point regarding potential; Nigeria had the potential to be one of the greatest countries in the world, a showcase and celebration of Black excellence, achievement and education, instead we are the laughing stock of the world, forced to live in foreign countries bearing the brunt of racism, racial profiling and racial stereotyping. We also have to be wary of not getting caught up in Black on Black violence.

A country that could have elevated the status of Black people around the world and help Black people to be seen in a positive light has failed to deliver and has helped to reinforce the stereotypes people have of Black people and Africans.

It doesn't take a genius to understand that education and

economic development go hand in hand, but in many respects it probably does. We see countries like the UK and US relying on past glory not really understanding that the game has changed and that countries like Finland and Singapore are leaving them trailing behind. The same applies to Nigeria; myopic and illiterate leaders have failed to invest in education or anything for that matter, rather searching for new and inventive ways to destroy the country.

Singapore became an independent nation in 1965 and unlike Nigeria had very few natural resources, successive governments chose to invest in education and today Singapore has jumped from a third world nation to first world nation in terms of education.

Nigeria gained independence in 1960 and went from an agrarian society to one that is now dependent on revenue from petroleum. Unlike Singapore, Nigeria went from a nation with promise to a third world country to a failed state and will continue to descend into further depths of hopelessness.

The Olympics of 2012 will probably go down in history as one of the best, while some in the British media were complaining about "plastic Brits" (athletes representing Britain, who weren't born in the UK but became eligible to represent Britain), many Nigerians or athletes of Nigerian origin were forced to represent nations other than the ones of their birth, Fiji, even fielded a "Nigerian" athlete.

If Nigeria was any good or had good governance, rather than allowing for money to be stolen. If money was invested in sports facilities, infrastructure etc., parents of children who showed potential in sports would probably have stayed in the country rather than having to leave and relocate to countries where sport is taken more seriously.

A country of 160 million people failed to win a single medal at the Olympics. Shameful does not even qualify their performance, however, the athletes cannot be blamed as such for the lack of medals won. The lack of sponsorship or facilities doesn't really help.

Who knows. If Nigeria had utilised it's potential, the likes of Phillips Idowu, Andrew Osagie and Christine Ohurogu could have worn the green, white and green of Nigeria.

Against all odds, Nigeria continues to produce highly skilled and qualified individuals who can compete on the world stage but because of the greed and narrow mindedness of those in power, these people either have to leave the country en masse or become another statistic in Nigeria's ever increasing production line of wasted talent. No other country in the world allows it's best and brightest to leave or just rot. If Nigeria invested in education like countries like Finland or Singapore, Nigeria really would be the greatest country on Earth.

As of January 2013, France is currently involved in a military campaign to help defeat Islamic extremists in Mali, one of its former colonies. A military force is also expected from some other West African states, Nigeria being one of them. One of the reasons France had to intervene is that Mali does not have the military capability to defeat the extremists. Nigeria, as is being reported, will contribute 1200 soldiers, but the story is the same, the soldiers are poorly equipped and are being sent into a conflict they can barely have an impact in.

It is quite embarrassing that France can put a fighting force together within a matter of days and within hours arrive from Europe and engage in battle with an enemy. Neighbouring West African countries are just about getting troops together, days after the French have launched aerial strikes and bombarded enemy positions as well as having engaged in street battles.

Nigeria, like many third world countries, has used its army to brutalise it's civilian population and stage coup after coup, yet when the army is called upon to carry out its primary purpose, it is found wanting. Many Nigerian Generals are multi-millionaires living in opulence and yet they are proud to preside over a fighting force that is impotent. If any European power decided that it wanted to take over Nigeria, the exercise would probably be over in a week. We have a military that cannot carry out its primary objective, to defend its citizenry from external aggression. The notion of sovereignty and independence for Nigeria and most African countries is really a joke.

As of 2015, Nigeria is now (the North at present) battling against Boko Haram a fanatical Islamist sect that is wishing to impose Sharia law across the country. Many of the stories that are emerging from Nigeria are quite disheartening, such as soldiers having only 60 bullets each to fight against an enemy that has much more superior fire power than the Nigerian soldiers. Some soldiers do not have a uniform, they have had to buy their kit from their own money. Rather than being a professional fighting force which any national army is meant to be, they are a depleted, spent force. It is hard to believe that Nigeria spends four billion dollars a year on defence.

Some reports have also stated that some Nigerian soldiers are now deserting once they engage the enemy.

It is quite ironic that many thousands of Nigerians have been killed by other Nigerians wishing to impose a way of life and religion that is foreign to both Nigeria and Africa.

Can things change in Nigeria for the better, I really hope so, however, some of the values that many of us as Nigerians have – selfishness and the love of money – have to give way to selflessness and the love for one another.

There are many Nigerians living in the Diaspora who have the skills, knowledge and talent to make Nigeria the country we as Nigerians think and know it should be, however, the change that is needed will not occur if we continue on the current path we are on.

CHAPTER TEN

The re-election of Barack Obama as President of the United States was not only a truly historic moment, it was also a representation of so many things. It was the triumph of progress, fair play and change over extremism, bigotry and racism. It was and is a notice to America that it is time to change.

As is said, old habits die hard, any time Obama has made any mention or alluded to anything to do with his race, he has been met with a very negative reaction. Two examples come to mind, one being the arrest of Henry Louis Gates, the African-American professor who was arrested for "breaking into" his own home. Obama took a lot of flak for saying that the police were stupid to arrest Gates. With the shooting of Trayvon Martin, Obama again took a lot of flak for saying that if he had a son, he would probably look like Trayvon; the racists and bigots came out in force.

Since 1776, White males have been elected as Presidents of the United States of America, suddenly, a person of colour is in charge for eight years out of two hundred and thirty six years and suddenly there is a hue and cry. Statements such as "it's not a traditional America anymore" have been made. No truer statement could not have been made, imagine how Native American Indians felt when suddenly their land and country was taken from them by force. Unless, you are Native American Indian, you are an immigrant, legal or illegal, where a traditional American is concerned.

As was often said to immigrants in the UK, "if you don't like it here, you can go back to where you came from" – it was often put in much more colourful language – the same applies to those "Americans" who are unhappy with the change that has occurred/that is occurring. If you are not happy, go back to where you came from or where your ancestors came from. America is a melting pot of so many cultures, communities and people, each having contributed to the America as we now know it today, no one community has a God given right to be in control or have power indefinitely.

Obama's re-election showed that change has to come, nothing stays the same forever, even with his re-election, America's ugly past still surfaced, many racist tweets on Twitter were sent, showing that America still has a lot of work to do where racism is concerned. Obama has been questioned on his patriotism, his nationality and his educational qualifications, no other American President has had to endure such crude and disgusting attempts to pull them down. However, with dignity, professionalism and class, he has dealt with all the attacks.

Obama's re-election shows that America is changing. Mitt Romney's 47% quote will probably haunt him for a long time, but it was probably an indication of what he really thought, any representative of people has to represent all the people, irrespective of whether you share their beliefs or not (when I say beliefs, I mean beliefs that are legal). The Republican Party thought that its base was strong enough to elect and represent an America that looked like 1964.

I am not sure if America will ever have another Black President, however if anyone was ever going to be that person, Obama was the perfect candidate.

As I have always said, for us as Black people as the status quo stands for now, we have to adopt a position of duality. Obama does that perfectly, he is able to navigate between both the Black world and White world effortlessly, he has also had an international upbringing. No White politician can truly understand the needs or the daily challenges of a person of colour.

Obama understands and lives in both worlds and has been able to amalgamate the two. It is often said that when Obama addresses different audiences, depending on the make up of the crowd, he will adapt his way of speaking to that particular audience; see *Articulate While Black* by Alim H. Samy & Geneva Smitherman, that is the hallmark of a person who has a connection to the people. That is the beauty of Obama, he can mix with a labourer and show genuine concern and be at total ease as well as host a meeting of the heads of the G20 or NATO and display great leadership and conviction.

Apart from being the person that he is, progressive and forward thinking, Obama was able to win the election both in 2008 and 2012 by being smart. When I say smart, I am not talking about being smart in the academic way of talking, he has that in abundance, I mean being smart in knowing when to be "Black" and when to be "White".

Oftentimes when a Black person is speaking, be it a British person or an American, you can tell whether it is a Black person or a White person, some may say that is racist, however it is fact (note I said oftentimes not all the time). Certain phrases that are used also sometimes give the identity of the speaker away. Obama did not fit the stereotype of White America, his spoken English when addressing White America was impeccable and faultless. Here was a Black man who spoke "White American English" better than most White Americans, had the mannerisms of White America and did not sound Black.

Even though Black, Obama was "White" enough for those White Americans who had doubts and fears and "Black'" enough for those Black Americans who probably felt that he probably wasn't one of their own.

No other Head of State that I know of can cross so many boundaries, races, and religions as Obama can. A true representative of the people must have the ability to be able to relate to all people, not just a select privileged few.

Special praise and credit also needs to be given to Obama, no other Presidential candidate or President seeking re-election has had to work as hard as Obama. Being the only African-American President in America's history, Obama has had to get a high percentage vote from the majority, i.e, the White majority. In all other elections gone by, whether minorities voted or not, a White candidate always won and lip service could be paid to minorities to get their vote if a candidate wanted to appear as friendly towards minorities.

However, from 2016, the minority vote will now prove crucial in deciding who takes up residence in the White House.

Going forward, one has to ask how will White America respond if indeed it does become the minority in years to come. After Obama's re-election a petition signed by 100,000 people in Texas called for Texas to secede from the union of the United States. When George W. Bush won the 2000 election under contentious circumstances, people voiced their opinions, but still got on with things; I don't recall any states or people calling for an annexation from the union of the United States. I can only assume that if Obama was White, there may have been those unhappy with his re-election, but no one would be calling for a break up of the union.

I think what really galls those who are calling for a secession is that Obama has beaten them at their own game, i.e at the ballot box. For years, Blacks were denied the right to vote. The Voting Rights Act of 1965 finally gave Black people the right to vote; the democratic process that America is so quick to advocate for others is how Obama has come to power, however, as that Democracy has now produced a result that is not favourable to some, parts of America would rather go backward and not forward.

Whatever legacy Obama leaves behind, one thing that will remain incontrovertible is that Black people can do anything and become anything.

CHAPTER ELEVEN

How do we get Black people out of the downward spiral that too many Black people are caught up in? Throughout this book I have talked about the importance of education and I again go back to that point.

Apart from education a number of other factors will play a part, some of these points I will touch on this chapter such as knowing who we are as Black people, learning from history, being inspired by others and wanting to do great things amongst other things.

We are now living in a world that has changed so much within the last thirty to forty years. Gone are the days when you could leave school without any qualifications and get a job, the very few jobs of a manual capacity that are still available still require that people have a basic education, be it one O Level or so.

I am yet to see any job advertised stating that no education is required, an ad might state no experience needed, however, the assumption would be that even though the person applying for such a job had no experience, the applicant would have some sort of education. We live in a highly competitive technological age where education is a prerequisite for success.

A lot of our children are being left behind in this race, we might be consumers of the technology available, i.e. iPads, iPhones, flat screen TV's etc. but where are our kids when it comes to the invention or innovation of such products.

Until recently, I had never heard of Lonnie Johnson, as I am sure many people haven't either. Lonnie Johnson is an

African-American inventor and former NASA scientist. He is responsible for the invention of the super soaker water gun whose sales have now reached almost $1 billion. Needless to say Mr Johnson is a very rich man, but more importantly, he is a very intelligent man; he holds a Masters degree in Nuclear Engineering.

In the UK I cannot name any Black inventors or innovators, there might be some and they probably have not received any exposure, but I am not sure that is the case, even if it is the case, I doubt there are many. I hope that it is the latter, that there are some and they are just not yet well known. As I have stated previously, too many of our kids are too preoccupied by owning all the latest gadgets, being cool and not really having an understanding of the benefits of what a good education will bring.

My son went on a trial interview, he was in his penultimate year of secondary school, being born and bred in South London, he has a typical South London accent and is fifteen years old. Teenagers being who they are can tend to be lazy in their speech. Irrespective of what politicians may say; that we live in a democratic, free and fair society, we all know that is not the case. People automatically judge you on how you look, walk, talk etc. it's human nature to do so.

Both my wife and I were able to coach him on some basic interview tips and techniques, from giving a firm handshake to saying *yes* rather than *yeah* when responding to questions, to walking straight. To most people these are just basic things and common sense issues, however too many young people both Black and White do not even know these basic things and have no understanding of the impact of informal and formal speech.

Having completed the interview, a few weeks later we received feedback from the company via his school to say how pleased they were with him.

People generally, have lost the art of reading situations or are just so lacking in the understanding of the power of language. I have been in situations where a group of individuals has been addressed by a prospective client, job seeker etc. and the opening salutation is "Hi Guys" or " Hiya". If I am meeting people for the first time I will always start with Good Morning etc. I cannot say Hiya or Hi Guys to people that I have not met before or that I am not familiar with. I hate the excuse people give, that people are young and will change. I don't buy that, it's common sense and good manners. Amongst friends you can be that familiar, but not in a business meeting or job interview.

This is both a Black and White issue and it is hurting our kids. I remember a friend of mine whose son at the time was about seven or eight getting quite upset as she said that at times if she introduced her son to friends or colleagues he would say hello. She was of the opinion that he should say Good Morning, Good Afternoon or Good Evening even if the person he had been introduced to had said hello as their initial introduction.

Personally, I thought she was making a big deal of things, however, like many Black parents who have an understanding of how things really are, she wanted to make sure that her son was able to/would be able to navigate a society in which he would be judged on so many levels from his qualifications and his use of language to the colour of his skin.

I never cease to be amazed when I go into a shop and see young teenagers, sometimes even grown men asking the shopkeeper for something and saying "give me that" or "let me have that". Whatever happened to starting a sentence with "May I have" or "Can I have"? Please and thank you are also two words that are quite effective when interacting with other people. If you do not know how or refuse to communicate effectively or politely with people or fail to understand the power of words then you set yourself up to be disadvantaged.

Speaking properly is not about trying to be White, it is about being empowered and educated. If you are unable to communicate effectively, your options become even more limited. It really does amaze me that parents and schools are not doing anything to correct the way that children speak. I am not advocating that everyone speaks with a cut glass plummy accent. People should at least be able to get basic pronunciation right, nowadays, people speak in a sort of sing song way, all the wrong syllables are emphasised, statements and questions are no longer differentiated as the ability to make use of inflection has been lost.

I cannot over emphasise the importance of education enough, we now have a generation of children who are reliant on Google for all of their information, they can regurgitate and parrot the works of other people, but are unable to put anything in their own words. Even when things are put in their own words, the end result is often quite embarrassing.

A return to basic English is needed, people need to have a strong foundation in English, basic grammar needs to be taught and mastered. Statements like "he done well" need to be replaced with the correct tense, "he did well". "One of them apples" needs to be taught and corrected to "one of those apples".

What I find quite baffling at times is that Black people (not all) in America and UK live in societies where English is spoken, yet oftentimes Black people who are not indigenous to these places speak and write better English than UK and US Blacks.

The pressure to "look good" does not only apply to women, nowadays, you see a lot of men both Black and White with bulging muscles everywhere. It takes a lot of discipline and hard work to look how these people look.

I often find myself thinking, that if the Black men who look like super heroes spent the amount of time they do in the gym looking for work, raising their kids or pursuing education, maybe Black families might not be in the predicament that they are in today. If the same energy, drive and commitment could be put into other pursuits that would benefit us academically, professionally and economically, we would find ourselves in a better place. (This is not meant as a sweeping statement or characterisation, but there are a few people both Black and White who spend more time in the gym than with their kids.)

I mentioned earlier how, other groups in America have a sense of belonging when it comes to definition, i.e. Italian-American, Irish-Americans etc. Black people in America haven't had it quite straightforward, amongst other things we have been called coloured, Negro, Black and now African-American. Personally, I think African American is probably the best description, however, one has to ask, what is African about Black people in America today?

How many African-Americans have been to Africa, how many African-Americans can speak or even identify an African language? What traditions or cultures from Africa do today's Black people in America demonstrate?

With regards to African culture and traditions, Black America has fallen short, most African communities that haven't been diluted by Western culture place a great emphasis on respect and family. Black America unfortunately has not imbibed these practices. Today, the majority of Black children in America are born into single parent families with absent fathers and the concept of respect is in very short supply.

Slavery decimated Black families, however, sometimes, you have to be strong and decide to be different and make a difference. As a child, I witnessed domestic violence and a host of other ills, however, from a very early age I was resolute and made a decision that I wanted something better and would never indulge or engage in the things that I had experienced.

My point being is that we don't have to always be defined by our experiences or circumstances, especially if they are negative ones. We now live in a society where people taking responsibility for their actions is becoming the exception and not the norm. There is always a psychologist on hand to give a reason or explanation for the crimes, anti-social behaviour and lack of respect for those who want to live outside the realms of accepted behaviour.

In many respects it's quite funny how many children in America and the UK are now diagnosed with ADHD (Attention Deficit Hyperactivity Disorder). In the third world or developing world ADHD is almost unheard of. To me a lot of what passes off or is passed off as ADHD is probably just a lack of discipline and parental control. I don't doubt ADHD does exist, but not in the numbers that are presented to us.

It just seems funny that in a lot of societies and cultures that have become very liberal and adopted an almost laissez faire attitude to how children are raised/disciplined that these issues seem to now be a problem (I know that is a very controversial statement to make, but I can only say things as I see them).

Many people of my generation who are now in their 40s and 50s all have similar tales to tell with regards to discipline, sometimes the discipline did verge on cruelty and child abuse, or at least what would be termed child abuse by today's standards, which I am not advocating. However, it stood us in good stead, we had/have an understanding of what is wrong or right, we can cook, clean, we have respect for our colleagues, elders and we have a good work ethic.

These qualities weren't instilled into us in that our parents spoke to us on one occasion and we automatically took them to heart, sometimes we had to learn that there were consequences to not doing what we were told or for disrespecting our parents or elders, excuses were not made for our bad behaviour. An expectation was had that as children/young adults, we needed to have a sense of responsibility and be obedient to our elders, parents and conform to the rules of society.

I am not saying that everyone of my generation turned out to be angels or upstanding citizens, but we definitely had/have different standards of the youth of today. We didn't take drugs or guns to school and very few of us if any at all had killed anyone. We are all too quick to dispense with old fashioned values and oftentimes, what replaces the old fashioned values leads our children down a very slippery and dangerous path.

As far as the Black community is concerned, we need to revisit some of the things that worked for us because where we are today as a people and as a community is not where we should be. As mentioned previously, we are in a rapidly changing world, where education, the ability to speak foreign languages, a good work ethic are going to be prerequisites for success.

A lot of our children struggle to speak standard English, let alone have a grasp or a mastery of another language. We cannot continue to claim racism if we get left behind. Nobody will hand us anything on a plate. We will have to work hard for the things that we need and for the ability and opportunity to compete.

Slavery and colonialism did untold damage to Africa, but what did we learn from that? It would appear that African leaders have learnt nothing. They have learnt how to loot and suppress their people, but have not learnt how to develop or invest in their nations. Most African countries have extremely fertile land, but how many African countries are self-sufficient when it comes to food production? How many African countries can boast of good roads, clean water and constant electricity?

The scariest thought of all is that if the West wanted to recolonise Africa, what would stand in their way? Apart from South Africa, I cannot think of any African nation that can defend itself militarily from any Western power, let alone any Eastern European nation. South Africa excluded, I don't think any other African nation develops or produces any ammunition or armaments of any kind. Our armies are ill equipped, often lack discipline, have the most basic of equipment and have no real experience of warfare per se.

We have no submarines to guard or patrol our International waters, we have no aircraft carriers, our airforces are barely operational. What stands in the way of Africa being recolonised?

If African leaders really gave thought to such things, they wouldn't spend their time amassing fortunes in Swiss bank accounts and running their countries into the ground.

China is now the new face of technical expertise and financial benevolence in Africa. Great things are being done, however, it would be naive to think that all of China's actions are totally altruistic. Africa needs to get to a position where it is self-sufficient in all aspects, otherwise, she will just be exploited as in previous times, but in a more subtle way.

We as Black people need to carve out a new definition of what it means to be Black, as with many things, the current definition of what it means to be Black has been hijacked by both the Black and White community. Just as difficult as it is to define what it means to be White, the same needs to be the case as to define what it means to be Black.

Black "culture" should be seen to represent, amongst other things, progress, intelligence, sophistication. Positive images of

Black people need to be reinforced and projected by both the Black and White media. We have had our fill of Black people who are hip, cool, sassy or promiscuous, we want to see Black people who are excelling in the field of science, medicine, business, computing, space exploration etc.

If our role models are just rappers and football players, then we will continue to struggle for a long time as the world needs more than just footballers and rappers. Rappers and footballers do not teach, they cannot deliver babies, they do not contribute to scientific breakthroughs. They are good at what they do, but in the grand scheme of things in regards to what the world needs to continue to function and progress, their contribution isn't really that great.

With regards to unity and working together, Black people have a bit of work to do. I do get annoyed when some Black people refer to other Black people as "coconuts" or any other stupid derogatory term when someone who does not conform to their definition of "Blackness" comes along. Coconut being used to refer to a Black person who is trying to "act White", acting White usually means speaking properly, being professional and being broad minded.

What I do have a problem with is Black people who having reached a certain position or station in life and feel that they have a point to prove to their boss(es) and feel that they have to be harder on other Black members of staff to prove to their bosses that they know how to handle "unruly Black people".

To try and fit in, they feel like they have to almost deny all trace of their "Blackness" and by "Blackness" I don't mean all the negative connotations that go with being Black, but being true to themselves.

Personally speaking, in the work environment, I have on some occasions found some of my bosses who have happened to be Black to be the worst; they have deliberately marked me down in assessments. I had one boss, again who was Black, who said to me that I was not a typical Black man. I am not sure what he meant by that statement, but he chose not to clarify it and I did not choose to seek clarification (however I have an idea of what he meant).

On the flip side, the White bosses that I have had, generally have been very good. I have had some terrible ones as well. What it does show is that irrespective of colour, people are the same, you find good and bad in all races.

Black people should not feel the need to pull one another down to prove a point. If you are fair consistent and knowledgeable in what you do, everything else will take care of itself.

As I have mentioned earlier in most African societies, family is of great importance. Birth, marriages and deaths are of equal if not greater importance. Amongst the Yoruba of Nigeria, the birth of a child is a cause for great celebration, the child is given a name on the eighth day, friends and family are called to join in the celebration of the naming of the child. Not only is the child named, the child is prayed for. Names for Africans are of great importance and Yoruba children usually have a name given by the parents and grandparents.

Our names are profound and rich in meaning. My name, for instance, means, came with wealth; my surname in many respects is a warning, loosely translated means that the god of iron/war will take vengeance on my behalf.

Male children are also circumcised on the eighth day, some have claimed that the Yoruba originally came from Egypt and this was a practise that arrived with the new arrivals from Egypt. From a hygiene point of view, we are all aware of the benefits of circumcision. In some respects I suppose that is why Nigerians, especially the Yoruba are extremely confident, some may say arrogant. We are acutely aware of our heritage, culture, tradition and language and believe we can do anything

As Black people or Africans, we need to be a bit more discernible as to what works for us. In the west, oftentimes the focus is on money, wealth and prestige which is in itself not intrinsically wrong, however, we now have a generation of people who want the very finest of what life has to offer without putting in the hard work that is required.

Many teenagers in the West now live a life that their parents could never have dreamed of, but yet are still generally unhappy, moody and at times suicidal.

In the developing world many kids do not have Xboxs, Playstations and all the other mod cons of modern life, but with the little they have, they are happy, content and sociable.

I can remember as a young teenager in Lagos watching young kids with just a tyre and a stick used to roll a tyre up and down the street having hours of fun and hearing laughter from the very core of their souls.

Some of the most joyful of people that I have met are those who have very little, even with the little they have they are still willing to share what they have. Yet a lot of people who are quite well off have a host of issues, depression, substance abuse issues, dysfunctional relationships, body image issues, the list goes on and on. Life in the West isn't always what people would have us believe.

Unless there is a war going on, no one in a traditional society would wake up, go to school and massacre their class mates. It's just unheard of, yet in times of peace, it is becoming more and more the norm for school kids in the West to go to school and murder their colleagues. Parental authority in the West has been totally eroded and parents no longer have the ability or authority to control their children.

When communities and societies abandon what has

worked for them, rot, disintegration and finally collapse sets in. In recent times, strong societies and communities had certain things in common, a sense of morality, Church/religion and a strong work ethic. In the West we have now dispensed with the above and a very gradual, yet noticeable decline has set in.

The majority of my secondary school education was in Lagos. I would have to catch the bus to and from school. The nearest bus stop to our house was about a quarter of a mile's walk from where we lived. From the time I left my house to the time I reached the bus stop, I would always meet someone who knew my father. If I failed to greet anyone that I encountered and word got back to my father, I would be in trouble. As far as my father was concerned I, as his child, was a reflection and representative of him and like most Nigerian parents, he did not want to be seen in a negative light. Good manners therefore always had to be at the forefront of everything we did.

Today, in the West, it is not unheard of for people to not even know who their next door neighbours are, let alone know who lives on their street or apartment complex. There are many instances where people have passed away in their homes and have not been discovered for a considerable length of time due to the very isolated life style that people can have in the West.

Every year, we seem to push the boundaries as to how much naked flesh we can show on TV or how many obscenities we can squeeze into sentences that are grammatically incorrect. People are happy to not be in employment and to be seen drunk in public and use expletives in every area of public life, i.e. at work, on public transport etc. To be different is almost now viewed as being a bit weird, strange or even snobbish.

In his book *Coming Apart,* Charles Murray discusses the

decline in American values. However, his observations should not be limited to just America as the West seems to always take its lead from America. Many of the points raised do not just relate to America, they relate to many industrialised countries as well.

Black people living in the West and America generally are assimilated and acculturated into the societies they live in and also face racism, poor education, limited opportunities, poor housing and above average single parent households. Is it any wonder that many people view Black people as problem people? In some respects, they suffer more, apart from the problems that having Black skin can bring in countries where that skin colour is not the majority, they are also affected by all the social problems that these Western nations also suffer from.

In recent times, America has launched a war against drugs and terror. Western nations have followed suit, but really what is needed is a war against ignorance, a desire to get something for nothing, stupidity, broken homes and sexual crimes against children, to name a few.

Western nations will not be brought down by Islamic extremists or drugs, though these things will have an impact and cannot be allowed to go unchecked. What will bring Western nations down is the paths they have now chosen to go down where the above have been allowed to fester for too long.

The role of women in helping to bring about a change in the Black community cannot be over-emphasised. Too many woman have settled for anything that presents itself as a man and are willing to settle down or have a child or children with someone who has no employment history, has no legitimate income, has several unsupported children from various relationships and still thinks that wearing sagging trousers is a fashion statement.

If Black women did not give these men the time of day,

they would soon have to change and become men in character and conduct, not just in reproductive capabilities. Too many Black women are afraid of being alone or left on the shelf that they will settle for anyone that shows up in a pair of trousers that comes along and start a "family" with these characters.

Black women need to be a bit more selective at times in choosing who to settle down with. We all talk about Obama, however, if Obama was not up to scratch, there is no way that his wife would have paid any attention to him.

It's not about being snobbish or superior, it's about knowing one's self-worth and about having standards. It's often said, you can't lie down with a dog and not catch fleas, the same applies in this sense, you can't hook up with a ghetto man or woman and not take on some of their ways. I suspect that this might be the real reason why a lot of accomplished Black women are settling down with White men.

Why would a woman who knows her worth want to settle down with a man who cannot hold down a job? It is definitely not a matter of being snobbish, even if Black women cannot find a mate who matches them academically, I am sure they would settle for someone who is reliable, dependable, mature and who has a job and doesn't have several children who are not catered for.

Like usually attracts like, if someone is educated, decent, and financially stable, they tend to look for similar qualities in a mate.

Sometimes, I think we have to be a bit smart and not take on all the mixed messages that are sent out. Today, the number of single parent households in the west have exploded. There is nothing intrinsically wrong with a single parent household, however you don't have to be a genius to know that children growing up in a two parent household tend to fare better.

Whether knowingly or unknowingly, a lot of Black women

have bought into this and we have a lot of antagonism between Black men and women, with a lot of women claiming they don't need a man (which, if he was a waste of space would be true).

We have a lot of fatherless Black households where children are growing up without any guidance, instruction or discipline.

If we look at those who wield power, their family structure tends to be what we would describe as the traditional family set up, two parents and usually married.

Take the royal family for instance, even though they are connecting to the general populace even more, certain things do not change, where there is a marriage, the marriage usually happens first and then children come along. We don't seem to have children being born out of wedlock (though in the past, in centuries gone by that might not have always been the case), the same applies to a lot of educated middle-class families and professionals, they tend to get married first and then have kids. Many gay couples too, now adopt children as they know as a two parent family they can offer their children more.

As Black people, we need to be a bit more discerning where the structure of family is concerned, we need to ensure that our kids are able to set out on as firm a foot as possible, i.e. a structured and strong(er) family set up.

Even if a lot of White people do go down the single parent route, more often than not, they still have a sort of safety net to fall back on – parents, grandparents etc. Most immigrant families as far as Britain is concerned are second or third generation and are not as established as the indigenous population. i.e. many Whites can rely on mum and dad to help with a deposit or large cash injection to buy their first car or house.

As the children of immigrants, many of us do not have that luxury, our parents were not that established in society and after about 15-20 years after their initial arrival returned home with their children.

We the children of these immigrants who had gone back home, would now make the same journey that our parents had made in the 50s and 60s, the difference being that this time, we came back as citizens.

We were armed in many cases with our degrees which were often frowned upon or not even rated, but that didn't deter us. Many of us just went and got a Masters or a Doctorate. For those that did not come back with a degree, they came with a strong work ethic and a desire and drive to succeed.

As a people, Nigerians are extremely ambitious and industrious, however, when we hear stories about Nigerians, we never hear about these qualities, we hear about credit card scams etc., but the drive, resilience and excellence of Nigerians is never touched upon. Europeans/Whites have a propensity for certain crimes, yet we do not judge the whole of Europe by the crimes that some commit, we judge the individual. As Black people, we haven't as yet been afforded that luxury.

On one hand, we decry the sexualisation of our children, yet we have no issue giving girls as young as twelve the pill in school without the knowledge or consent of parents. We claim that we want our children, role models and "celebrities" to be well behaved, but when they are, they are termed boring. If they are badly behaved, they are condemned. Is it any wonder we have a generation of children growing up confused?

The message for Black people should be, because something is permissible, it does not mean that it is always beneficial.

As mentioned earlier the slave trade did untold damage to African communities and to Africans in the Diaspora, effects of which are still being felt today. People who do not have an understanding of what the slave trade did or it's effects will now say that slavery ended over two hundred years ago and that it is now time for Africans and Black people to stand on their own feet.

The strange thing with regards to the Slave Trade is that many people are completely ignorant to what it actually represented, aside from it being one of the darkest times in human history, it was also a licence for murder, rape, paedophilia and other unspeakable crimes to be carried out by one human being to another without any repercussions or consequences.

The Civil Rights movement has come a long way since the 60s, however, there now seems to be a lethargy and at times indifference to the plight of Black people as people believe that 50+ years is now time enough for people of colour to have risen to an equal/level footing in society.

Times are changing and different battles are being fought, i.e. women's rights, gay rights. Tomorrow, it could be the rights of those wishing to practise polygamy or polyandry. While there is still some understanding and sympathy to our plight, Black people need to make the most of all the opportunities that life presents, otherwise we will be left behind.

We could find ourselves in a situation where people say that Black people have had a helping hand for so long and nothing has really changed and a hardened attitude is formed towards those who do require help and support. The tide does seem to be changing. A recent survey in America held by the Pew Research Centre found that 63% of Americans felt that African-Americans were responsible for their inability to succeed.

A rethink needs to be had as to what our values are, who our role models are and how we can enrich and strengthen our communities. The new "values" we have adopted have not helped us in the slightest, we have high levels of incarceration, high levels of exclusion from schools, ever increasing single parent households, high drug dependency levels, high levels of illiteracy, ever increasing levels of mortality and yet we persist in the lifestyle that has nothing to offer, other than a one way ticket to the morgue or prison.

We have reached a position whereby we can no longer deceive ourselves and say that there isn't a problem, but there is still a reluctance by both the Black and White community to deal with the issues that have arisen. Not every White person can afford to move out of the inner cities or live in gated-off communities and not every Black person can afford to live in an affluent area that has a low crime level.

The things that held us together as Black people were not take away from us as such, we gave them up voluntarily, we gave up our pride and dignity, we gave up our work ethic and we gave up our thirst for knowledge and education. We gave up our respect for one another and good manners.

In recent years, America has seen a number of shootings in schools (from Columbine to the most recent Sandy Hook) where White boys have gone into schools and slaughtered their class mates. Often times, the carnage has been explained away as the perpetrators having suffered from some sort of mental illness or psychosis.

If the shoe were on the other foot and the gunmen happened to be Black, we would not be talking about mental illness, psychosis or troubled family lives, we would hear things like the Black male has an innate drive within his psyche to be violent or that he has a propensity or proclivity towards criminal activity.

Since all these massacres, one has to ask why we have not applied the term "White on White" crime to such events. If that were to happen it would pre-suppose that White people have the same tendencies as any other ethnicity to carry out abhorrent and unforgivable crimes.

I suppose it's always easier to blame others for all the ills that society faces, immigrants, illegals and others who do not conform to the description of what "Real Americans" look like.

With a lot of the problems that the Black community faces and suffers from, when these problems are discussed, the term "Black Culture" is often applied. What is this Black Culture that people refer to? As a Black man, what is often described and portrayed is often alien to me.

Such terms, I find, are most unhelpful. Black culture would mean different things to a Nigerian, Afro-Brazilian and someone from Guadeloupe.

Rather than trying to infer that certain cultures have a disposition to crime or committing certain crimes, common sense shows that mankind, irrespective of colour is capable of great evil.

I probably sound like a broken record, but I have to go back again to the emphasis on education. Recently, I came across an article about Ben Carson. Dr. Ben Carson was, until his retirement recently, probably one of the most brilliant paediatric brain surgeons in America. What made his story so remarkable was that he had every reason not to be successful, he was raised in a single parent family, he was not brilliant at school, in fact he was labelled the class dummy and he was Black and also grew up in poverty.

How did he get from being the class dummy to being one of the most preeminent brain surgeons in the world? Once his mother realised that his grades in school were slipping, she introduced new rules into the household. Ben and his brother were only allowed to watch two programmes on TV a week and they also had to read two books a week from the library and give a written overview of what they had read.

Within the space of about a year and a half, the class "dummy" had suddenly become one of the best students in the class, if not the best student in the class, the rest as they say is history.

Ever since, I heard about this man, I have been like a man possessed, I have read two of his books, I have watched the film about his life story and have also given one of his books *Gifted Hands* to my son to read and to a work colleague to read.

His life story and rise to success are inspirational and are truly amazing. His mother was smart enough to realise that knowledge is power and that education unlocks the door to unlimited potential. His story also indicates that you do not have to allow your circumstances to define you, you can overcome your circumstances and become whatever you want to be.

Having read his story, I also came across an article about another brain surgeon, Dr. Keith Black, who also happens to be Black and is also highly celebrated. I have ordered a book about his life story from Amazon and await to be equally inspired upon reading it. These two men have done amazing things in their area of expertise. Again, it made me think, despite all the issues of race that abound in America, these two men were able to excel and become one of the best, if not the best in their field. The UK, on the other hand, which on the surface appears to have better race relations than the US, would not be the place where a Black man could become head of a department for neurosurgery. I doubt that we even have any Black brain surgeons in this country.

Many factors such as elitism and institutional racism amongst others prevent many minorities from progressing in the fields of Medicine and Law in the UK.

Having been inspired and encouraged by the examples of Dr Carson and Dr Black I could only laugh and also groan in despair after reading another story about a 15-year-old boy in

America (I believe in New York). The young man apparently had jumped a queue of people who were waiting to buy sneakers at $250 a pair. The person who he jumped in front of did not take too kindly to this, especially when the young man also began to get a bit mouthy. To cut a long story short, the aggrieved man left the queue only to return with a loaded gun and shot the queue jumper in the foot.

Many of the comments that people posted about the story rang so true. One person wrote, "where are the queues for people waiting to go into libraries", another wrote, "where is the equity in a pair of $250 pair of sneakers".

Aside from the young man who got shot, one has to ask, all the other people that were also queuing to spend a large amount of money on footwear, apart from looking cool, what other benefit would this pair of sneakers have brought them? $250 invested today will have some sort of return in ten years time. I doubt in ten years time that those sneakers that the young man got himself shot for will be worth that much, especially if they have been worn.

On a more positive note, in their book, *The Triple Package,* Amy Chua and Jed Rubenfeld discuss how certain groups in American seem to excel, whereas some don't.

One of the groups mentioned is Nigerians. According to them, Nigerians make up about 10% of all Black physicians in America. Nigerians are also over-represented in the field of Law and investment banking. To those of us who are Nigerians and have been privileged to experience and live the Nigerian experience it comes as no surprise.

Even with the dire state of a lot of schools in Nigeria now, Nigerians continue to excel as we have a can do attitude and have a thirst for knowledge and education. Even in families where both parents may be uneducated, children still go on and achieve great things educationally.

For real change and progress to come for Black people, we need for more than just certain groups or pockets of people to perform or excel, excellence needs to be the expectation and the norm.

The current "standards" that too many of us as Black people have for ourselves are not working; no society or community can thrive when there is an excess or over-representation of drugs, guns, fatherless households, teenage pregnancies, illiteracy and under-achievement.

If we can continue to pursue education, learn from our history, be inspired by the ever increasing pool of Black talent and have a greater belief in our self-worth, things will get better on a much larger scale.

CHAPTER TWELVE

What can bring about a change for Black people? I have talked a lot about education and I will go back to that again. Education does not have to end once you leave school. Even if you do not get the grades you need first time around, you can always retake your exams at college or go to night school. Adult Education classes are also there for the more mature student. Even as a mother to two children, one of whom is severely disabled, my wife managed to do a course in book keeping and also study and qualify as a homeopath. She also took courses in reiki healing and EFT. The point being that it is never too late to study despite what obstacles may seem to be in your way.

Dealing with emotions is another big thing, too many people today, both Black and White are angry for no just reason. People are too quick to get angry about the most trivial of things and oftentimes the consequences can be devastating. We live in a very macho culture for men, especially Black men and it is not seen as cool to talk about feelings or show emotions.

Emotions are very powerful feelings and they need to be expressed, be it in writing or verbally, however, if you do not have the skills to express yourself in either fashion, violence and rage are usually the only other option. I often have to use public transport and, being what it is, it requires that a lot of people are crammed into very tight fitting spaces. My experience is usually if someone accidentally treads on my foot, they usually either pretend that the incident did not happen, try and stare me down or apologise. Most of the time women will apologise, but for the men it is as if an apology is a sign of weakness and somehow their masculinity is compromised if an apology is given.

Self-respect and expectations are paramount in being able to lay the foundations for success in life. Self-respect encompasses so many things, from coming to work on time, providing for yourself and your family if you have one through legitimate means, to not fighting and cursing in the street. If you do not respect yourself, you cannot expect others to respect you.

What expectations do you have for yourself? A lot of people come from difficult backgrounds, but rather than use their difficult background to justify delinquency or anti-social behaviour, they use their difficult background to spur themselves on to greater things. From people like Dr Ben Carson to the average man or woman who despite various difficulties still manages to conduct themselves with class and dignity. They are the real heroes, not the reality T.V. celebrities that too many of us as Black people have come to embrace.

Determination is a great quality to have and is a quality that is needed to excel. You should never allow anyone to tell you that you cannot do something. I can remember studying for my O Levels in Nigeria. I was determined to do well as I knew getting my O Levels would be the first step with regards to furthering my education.

There were many factors against me; a home environment where my mother was absent, constant power cuts, various household chores such as waking up at 5am to fetch water as the house had no running water amongst other things. However, I was determined to not let anything stand in my way. In my final year of secondary school, I would study and revise from 2am-5am. If there was no electricity I would use a candle or hurricane lantern. For many in Nigeria, failure is not an option.

It is often said, no man is an island and it is true, in our daily lives, we all have to interact with people. Being respectful to people is not being soft, it shows that you have been brought up well. We all like to be treated respectfully, however, you usually get what you put out, if you put out attitude, you usually get back attitude, if you are polite and respectful, that is what you normally receive in return.

Learn the power of language and the difference between formal and informal speech. Some people answer the phone with "Who is this?" "May I know who is speaking?", or "Can I ask who is speaking, please?" sets a totally different and non-confrontational tone to the conversation. Language is extremely powerful and depending on how you use it, it can determine so many things from someone wanting to help you to getting or not getting a promotion.

For Black boys and girls to do well, sometimes a change of environment is what is needed for a fresh start. It could be moving to a different town to moving to a different country. Like a lot of people I know, a fresh start was also what I needed. In some cases, Black people that have done well are those who have spent part of their lives outside of the UK. In a lot of cases they have endured and encountered real hardship and poverty and have decided to not be another statistic.

Reading is also a key component to success, not only does it broaden your horizons, it helps to broaden and increase your vocabulary. Books are more important than the latest trainers or iPhone. Knowledge is power. Read autobiographies of people who have made it. I recently read the autobiographies of Colin Powell and Sir Alex Ferguson. Most people that have made it usually have followed a common path, one of hardship, difficulty and perseverance and finally success.

Dressing well is also of great importance. The way you dress sends a message to people of how you want to be perceived. You might be a cardiologist in your day job, however if you are dressed in sagging jeans, a hoodie and a bandanna, people will automatically assume you are a bad boy or thug. People have the right to wear what they want, however, sometimes misconceptions can be dealt with if people choose a different mode of dressing, a smart shirt and trousers worn properly sends out a different message than sagging jeans.

Cohesiveness is something that we in the Black community need to get back to. We are too fragmented and this is of our making to a certain extent. Yes, Europeans may have come to Africa and drawn up all kinds of artificial boundaries and borders, however as Black people and Africans, we have more similarities than dissimilarities. We need to look at the things that we have in common as Black people and work on those things to progress. We cannot blame White people for the distrust and animosity that exists at times amongst some Africans and West Indians towards one another (thankfully things are changing on that front and a lot more Africans and West Indians are now marrying each other).

Many years ago I met a lovely West Indian lady in my local laundrette and she told me that when West Indians first came to the U.K. many were able to buy houses and property due to the "partner" way of saving money, she lamented on how things are so different today, that you couldn't really trust people anymore to enter into such arrangements. We need to be able to get back to situations like that where we could rely on one another for help and support.

The "my brother's keeper" initiative launched in America by President Obama in 2014 is aimed primarily at young African-American males. The initiative has six main aims, some of which are that all youth remain free from violent crime, all youth complete post-secondary education or training, all children out of school are employed. The initiative is not about swag or looking cool or wearing sagging jeans, it's about education which enables people to become productive members of society and enables one to secure a decent job in the future.

Sooner or later, society will wake up and realise that a world class education is what is really needed to make a society develop and thrive, not reality TV stars and celebrities and when the time comes, my hope is that Black people will be there making incredible contributions.